Jeremy Diddler.

THE DIDDLER.

BY A. E. SENTER.

"Never you fear that, mun. I wasn't born two hundred miles north of Lunnun, to be done by Mr. Diddler, I know."—*Kenny's Farce of "Raising the Wind."*

NEW YORK:
M. DOOLADY, PUBLISHER,
448 BROOME STREET.
1868.

JOHN J. REED, PRINTER AND STEREOTYPER,
43 Centre Street, New York.

DEDICATION.

~~~~~~~~~~

To

THE LADIES AND GENTLEMEN,

MERCHANTS, BUSINESS MEN, MECHANICS AND LABORERS,

HUSBANDS AND WIVES,

CITIZENS OF THE UNITED STATES AND

PEOPLE OF THE WORLD,

GREETING :

To be posted and warned of the wiles of the DIDDLERS of our race, may save one from becoming their dupe, and, perhaps, from ruin.

'Where no counsel is, the people fall: but in the multitude of counsellors there is safety.''—PROV. xi. 14.

"A word to the wise is sufficient;" and to all others these pages are submitted.

By your humble servant,

A. E. S.
~~~~~~~~~~

NOTICE.

We would invite the attention of the reader to "Kenney's Farce of Raising the Wind," at the end of this volume. He will then be, if he is not already, familiar with Mr. Diddler, and perhaps better appreciate the main feature of this work.

PREFACE.

DIDDLING CONSIDERED AS ONE OF THE EXACT SCIENCES.*

"Hey, diddle diddle,
The cat and the fiddle."

SINCE the world began there have been two Jeremys. The one wrote a Jeremiad about usury, and was called Jeremy Bentham. He has been much admired by Mr. John Neal, and was a great man in a small way. The other gave name to the most important of the Exact Sciences, and was a great man in a great way—I may say, indeed, in the very greatest of ways.

Diddling—or the abstract idea conveyed by the verb to diddle—is sufficiently well understood. Yet the fact, the deed, the thing diddling, is somewhat difficult to define. We may get, however, at a tolerably distinct conception of the matter in hand, by defining—not the thing, diddling, in itself—but man, as an animal that diddles. Had Plato but hit upon this, he would have been spared the affront of the picked chicken.

Very pertinently it was demanded of Plato, why a picked chicken, which was clearly a "biped without feathers," was not, according to his own definition, a man? But I am not to be bothered by any similar query. Man is an animal that diddles, and there is no animal that diddles but man. It will take an entire hen-coop of picked chickens to get over that.

* We are indebted to the unknown author of this preface and other articles from his pen. May his shadow never grow less, and never be diddled worse.

What constitutes the essence, the nare, the principle of diddling is, in fact, peculiar to the class of creatures that wear coats and pantaloons. A crow thieves; a fox cheats; a weasel outwits; a man diddles. To diddle is his destiny. "Man was made to mourn," says the poet. But not so: he was made to diddle. This is his aim—his object—his end. And for this reason, when a man's diddled we say he's "done."

Diddling, rightly considered, is a compound, of which the ingredients are minuteness, interest, perseverance, ingenuity, audacity, nonchalance, originality, impertinence, and grin.

Minuteness: Your diddler is minute. His operations are upon a small scale. His business is retail, for cash, or approved paper at sight. Should he ever be tempted into magnificent speculation, he then, at once, loses his distinctive features, and becomes what we term "financier." This latter word conveys the diddling idea in every respect, except that of magnitude. A diddler may thus be regarded as a banker in petto—a "financial operation," as a diddle at Bobdignag. The one is to the other as Homer to "Flaccus"—as Mastodon to a mouse—as the tail of a comet to that of a pig.

Interest: Your diddler is guided by self-interest. He scorns to diddle for the mere sake of the diddle. He has an object in view—his pocket—and yours. He regards always the main chance. He looks to Number One. You are Number Two, and must look to yourself.

Perseverance: Your diddler perseveres. He is not readily discouraged. Should even the banks break, he cares nothing about it. He steadily pursues his end, and

Ut canis a cario nunquam absferrebitur uncto,

so he never lets go off his game.

Ingenuity: Your diddler is ingenious. He has constructiveness large. He understands plot. He invents and circumvents. Were he not Alexander, he would be Diogenes. Were he not a diddler, he would be a maker of patent rat-traps or an angler for trout.

Audacity: Your diddler is audacious. He is a bold man. He carries the war into Africa. He conquers all by assault. He would not fear the daggers of the Frey Herren. With a little more prudence, Dick Turpin would have made a good diddler; with a trifle less blarney, Daniel O'Connell; with a pound or two more brains, Charles XII.

Nonchalance: Your diddler is nonchalant. He is not at all nervous. He is never put out—unless put out of doors. He is cool—cool as a cucumber. He is calm—"calm as a smile from Lady Bury." He is easy—easy as an old glove, or the damsels of ancient Baiæ.

Originality: Your diddler is original—conscientiously so. His thoughts are his own. He would scorn to employ those of another. A stale trick is his aversion. He would return a purse, I am sure, upon discovering that he had obtained it by an unoriginal diddle.

Impertinence: Your diddler is impertinent. He swaggers. He sets his arms a-kimbo. He thrusts his hands in his trowsers' pockets. He sneers in your face. He treads on your corns. He eats your dinner; he drinks your wine; he borrows your money; he pulls your nose; he kicks your poodle, and he kisses your wife.

Grin: Your true diddler winds up all with a grin. But this nobody sees but himself. He grins when his daily work is done—when his allotted labors are accomplished—at night in his own closet, and altogether for his own private entertainment. He goes home. He locks his door. He divests himself of his clothes. He puts out his candle. He gets into bed. He places his head upon the pillow. All this done, and your diddler grins. There is no hypothesis. It is a matter of course. I reason *a priori*, and a diddle would be no diddle without a grin.

The origin of the diddle is referable to the infancy of the human race. Perhaps the first diddler was Adam. At all events, we can trace the science back to a very remote period of antiquity. The moderns, however, have brought it to a perfection never dreamed of by our thick-headed progenitors.

THE DIDDLER.

HOW PHIL MALOON RAISED THE WIND.

"There were at this muster one hundred at least,
Who were tipsy, or corned, or drunk as a beast;
There was old Rodney Hubbard and more I could name,
Who were ditto—yes, ditto—for ditto's the same."

YEARS ago, when the renowned muster days in New Hampshire—when men could get brutally intoxicated on five cents' worth of New England rum, and when heavy blows and sad discouragements were heaped upon the traffic in this beverage, there lived in the town of Ossipee, a man by the name of Philip Maloon, with an item or two in whose history we have something to do.

We live in comparatively moral times contrasted with those of 1851. It was then a law was passed, declaring the glorious truth, that "men are born free and equal" a nullity; for the unfortunate wight who happened to have a tinge—even the slightest—of Ethiopian blood in his veins, by that law was placed upon a level with the cattle and horses which might be taken to market and sold for a price. Upon the then existing state of things is the following story founded.

It was muster day at Ossipee, and Phil Maloon was there. If there was one thing above another that he religiously hated, that thing was work. He thoroughly detested that plebeian necessity. Running on errands, fishing, hunting, anything savoring of independent pleasure reconciled itself to Phil's mind ; but working ! that was a matter he could never bend his mind or his back to. Independent poverty was his primary characteristic. True, some associated him with the final departure of certain sheep and fowls from his locality, no track whereof had been left ; but then, even as now, there were detractors in the world. Phil's ragged garb, the people also said, bespoke him as being of the non-respectables (and truth to say, he was a very scarecrow in that respect) ; but it was also then as it is now, a patent fact that a glossy coat often covered the back of the greatest rogue. In one respect, he was superior to a majority on the muster field ; he was the stoutest and among the bravest there. His thirst corresponded with his strength and valor ; and but for the want of ten cents, a quart of new rum and he would have been bosom friends that same morning.

It was with mingled feelings of hope and despair that Phil threaded the crowd assembled at Ossipee during the early hours. No hand-shaking of his, no implied promise of future service, no coaxing, begging, imploring, praying, were, singly or collectively, productive of ten, five, or three cents in the way of a loan ; he witnessed, with lacerated appetite, old and young among his acquaintances, getting gradually drunk, as the poet sings :

———" glorious,
O'er all the ills of life victorious."

And not one single drop had warmed his gullet, or threatened even to pass that capacious cavity. What was to be done? "*Necessitas non habet legem*," thought Phil; but his mind dictated the idea in pure Yankee English. While cogitating as deep as a mine, he ran across old Rodney Hubbard; they condoled with each other, smoked the mutual *duddheen*, Irish calumet, or abbreviated clay pipe, with fraternal gusto; but the great question of "raising the wind" remained insoluble. Phil's wrath arose because of failure.

"Talk of a free country!" he said, "what *are* freedom? Where are the uses of free institootions, schools an' town meetin's, besides banks and lunatic 'sylums, if a feller hain't got a dime in his pocket? Them's the nuts I should like our legislatoors to crack! Who are the freemen of this great and flourishing United States that is free and ekal with nary a red cent in his fob, or any bills or loose change about him? I would just like to know that, Rodney. I would just put it to any reasonable man whether or no a feller's to be taken or not to be taken at his word when he promises a day's work—the money down in advance. I say it's a rotten state of things as says he shan't, and he not have a dime in his wallet; and a man'd better be a nigger slave in Virginny or Churubusco as have the name of a free citizen, when he ain't nothing of the sort! Them is my declared sentiments on this here interesting occasion—darn'd if they isn't!"

Rodney coincided; he was too thirsty and chop-fallen to hazard his voice in more than simple assent. Both then lay down on the sward in solemn cogitation.

At last Rodney, out of the fulness of his heart, spoke as follows:—

"Phil, are you willing to become a real teetotal, bona fyde nigger and no mistake, jist for the matter of two hours or so?"

"For a life-time,—until the last Sunday-bell tolls its last lick, rather than suffer under these here institootions we see off there," said Phil, pointing toward the crowd at a distance.

"Look at Squire Rundlett; just see how he enjoys himself in the most blessedest, highest, jolliest state in all creation, and me laying here like a darned son of a — I don't know what. Who wouldn't rather be a nigger, as me?

"Answer me, ye shades of Gineral Washington, Bonnyparty, and old Rough and Ready, as ye look down from your spears and see me—*me*, Phil Malone, with nary a darned cent to bless me in giving away in charity. No; any one may dance the break-down hornpipe in any of my pockets, and not break his shins over one red coin. I'd rather go the nigger dodge ten thousand times, as stand this state of things; yes-sir-ee! It's ongodly; it's onhuman; it's onconstitutional: it's—it's—I say it's—by Jehosaphat, I say it's agin the law—darn'd if it ain't! Nigger is men and is cared for as men, and I isn't. That's the differ; and who wouldn't rather be a nigger as me? A nigger for two hours! Let me be forever hereafter as black as the ace of spades. Them's 'em."

* * * * * *

About an hour after this conversation, Rodney Hubbard and a certain United States Marshal might have been seen penetrating the woods about a mile from Ossipee; and, on their arriving at a certain point, creeping on hands and knees towards a clump of thick brush, in the centre of which lay, snugly wrapped up in a horse blanket (his face beautifully embrowned by the juice of alder bark), our excellent friend Phil. A better specimen of a fugitive slave could not have been *manufactured;* and Rodney Hubbard's information promised the U. S. official good interest for a five dollar investment in that article of enlightenment.

All unexpectedly the *pro tempore* mulatto was seized and bound; and in a few minutes afterwards he was on his way to the Court House at Ossipee; but Rodney had to be bribed with a three dollar bill as part of his promised reward ere he would lend his hand as co-custodian of the runaway slave. On the party's reaching the Court House, Rodney was soon nowhere, and Phil was thirsting after the denouement.

Another hour afterwards and an individual looking like the U. S. Deputy Marshal, in a towering passion, might have been seen leaving the same Court House followed by Phil, who waxed loud in favor of free institootions, and the protection they offered to personal liberty against fälse imprisonments, etc. It took at least a couple of dollars to shut Phil's mouth on that occasion—but shut it was at last.

Another hour afterwards, and the spot in the woods where the capture took place was vocal with the mirth of Phil and Rodney. They enjoyed themselves; for a demijohn of new rum stood (now and then) between them, as they drank the health of the Deputy:

"Here's a health to the 'Dep,' may his belly grow wide,
And always have lots of good liquor inside,
May it stick out each side, and stick out before,
Till he never can see his old legs any more."

AN ELABORATE DIDDLER.

A MIDDLE aged gentleman arrives in town from parts unknown. He is remarkably precise, cautious, staid, and deliberate in his demeanor. His dress is scrupulously neat, but plain, unostentatious. He wears a white cravat, an ample waistcoat, made with an eye to comfort alone ; thick soled cosy-looking shoes, and pantaloons without straps. He has the whole air, in fact, of your well-to-do, sober-sided, exact, and respectable "man of business," par excellence—one of the stern and outwardly hard, internally soft, sort of people that we see in the crack high comedies—fellows whose words are so many bonds, and who are noted for giving away guineas, in charity, with the one hand, while, in the way of mere bargain, they exact the uttermost fraction of a farthing with the other.

He makes much ado before he can get suited with a boarding-house. He dislikes children. He has been accustomed to quiet. His habits are methodical, and then he would prefer getting into a private and respectable small family, piously inclined. Terms, however, are no object,—only he must insist on settling his bill on the first of every month (it is now the second), and begs his landlady, when he finally obtains one to his mind, not on any account to forget his instructions upon this point, but to send in a bill and receipt, precisely at ten o'clock, on the first day of every month, and under no circumstances to put it off to the second.

These arrangements made, our man of business rents an office in a reputable rather than in a fashionable quarter of the town. There is nothing he more despises than pretence. "Where there is much show," he says, "there is seldom anything very solid behind," an observation which so profoundly impresses his landlady's fancy, that she makes a pencil memorandum of it forthwith, in her great family Bible, on the broad margin of the Proverbs of Solomon.

The next step is to advertise, after some such fashion as this, in the principal business six-pennies of the city, —the pennies are eschewed as not "respectable"—and as demanding payment for all advertisements in advance. Our man of business holds it as a point of his faith that work should never be paid for until done:

Wanted.—The Advertisers, being about to commence extensive business operations in this city, will require the services of three or four intelligent and competent clerks, to whom a liberal salary will be paid. The very best recommendations, not so much for capacity as for integrity, will be expected. Indeed, as the duties to be performed involve high responsibilities, and large amounts of money must necessarily pass through the hands of those engaged, it is deemed advisable to demand a deposit of fifty dollars from each clerk employed. No person need apply, therefore, who is not prepared to leave this sum in the possession of the advertisers, and who cannot furnish the most satisfactory testimonials of morality. Young gentlemen piously inclined will be preferred. Application should be made between the hours of 10 and 11 o'clock, A.M., and 4 and 5 P.M., of Messrs. Boggs, Hogs, Logs, Frogs & Co.,
No. 110 Dog Street.

By the thirty-first of the month this advertisement has brought to the office of Messrs. Boggs, Hogs, Logs, Frogs and Company, some fifteen or twenty young gentlemen piously inclined. But our man of business is in no hurry to conclude a contract with any—no man of business is *ever* precipitate—and it is not until the most rigid catechism in respect to the piety of each young gentleman's inclination, that his services are engaged, and his $50 receipted for, *just* by way of proper precaution on the part of the respectable firm of Boggs, Hogs, Logs, Frogs and Company. On the morning of the first day of the next month, the landlady does *not* present her bill according to promise—a piece of neglect for which the comfortable head of the house ending in *ogs* would no doubt have chided her severely, could he have been prevailed upon to remain in town a day or two for that purpose.

As it is, the constables have had a sad time of it, running hither and thither, and all they can do is to declare the man of business most emphatically a "hen knee high," by which some persons imagine them to imply that, in fact, he is n. e. i., by which again the very classical phrase, *non est inventus*, is supposed to be understood. In the meantime the young gentlemen, one and all, are somewhat less piously inclined than before, while the landlady purchases a shilling's worth of the best Indian rubber, and very carefully obliterates the pencil memorandum that some fool has made in her great family Bible, on the broad margin of the Proverbs of Solomon.

ASTONISHING GULLIBILITY.

A MAN DIDDLED OUT OF SIX THOUSAND DOLLARS.

A. A. Reeves, is a quiet, well-to-do farmer, living about six miles northwest of Sedalia, Mo., on the Georgetown road. By hard work and frugal living, he had acquired the farm upon which he resided, and about $1,000 in money. Week before last, however, he was victimized in an almost incredible manner to the extent of $6,000, an amount which it will perhaps take half the earnings of his lifetime to repay.

On Thursday, Aug. 1, a company of gipsies, consisting of three men and one woman, encamped near Mr. Reeves' house. The woman called on Mr. R. the same day, representing to him that she was a clairvoyant fortune-teller, and that she was endowed with a secret gift, which enabled her to reveal the past and future of all things sublunary. Furthermore, she informed Mr. R. that she was a spiritualist, and that the spirits had communicated to her the astounding fact that somewhere on his (Mr. R.'s) farm, immense quantities of gold and silver had been hidden by some one at a time "whence the memory of man runneth not to the contrary." The charming woman continued to visit Mr. R.'s house from day to day, and finally informed him that the spirits would not deign to tell where the treasure was deposited, unless she could be temporarily placed in possession of $6,000 with which to perform the necessary incantation. Strange as it may seem, Mr. Reeves gave credence to this story: the woman completely infatuated him, leading him whithersoever she would. He promised her that he would obtain the money ($6,000), and each swore the other to eternal secrecy. Mr. R. had $965 in his own possession, and he quietly borrowed enough from different members of his family to make up the thousand, without hinting the purpose for which he wanted it. He then came to Sedalia and mortgaged his farm to Mr. Reeve Hughes, to the amount of $5,000, payable in ninety days, at two and a half per cent. a month. He thereupon returned home, without informing any member of his family what his mission had been to Sedalia; stealthily met his enchantress and told her he was ready for the incantation. The woman took the money, made a roll of it, wrapped it securely in a piece of cotton cloth, and, as if to make assurance doubly sure, she then took a long string and tied it many times around the roll of money. She returned the next day, when the final ceremonies took place, which were to inevitably extort a revelation from the spirits as to the exact locality where the treasure was to be found.

She took Mr. Reeves into a room where there could be no witnesses of the mysterious conjurations, had him to stand in the centre of the floor, and with uplifted hands repeat the Lord's Prayer, while she, in possession of the package of money, performed evolutions round about him, mysteriously chanting during the time. The performance concluded, the woman placed what was ostensibly the package of money in one of Mr. R.'s hands, and charged him, at the peril of destroying the spell, not to let the package go out of that particular hand until he had hidden it in some safe and secret place, where, undisturbed, it was to remain for the period of four days, when Mr. R. was to go and get it, and meet his enchantress at a spring near by, when the two in company would proceed to the place where the hidden treasure was buried. Mr. R. obeyed these instructions strictly, telling no one of any part of the transactions, hid what he supposed was his package of $6,000 safely away, and at the exact moment, when the four days expired, sought his package and found it, but alas! instead of containing the $6,000, it only contained the disconnected fragments of one of Beadle's Dime Novels!

The reader can imagine Mr. B.'s feeling of disappointment, indignation, and chagrin at this stage of the proceedings. He sought his charmer at the spring, but, alas! she was nowhere visible. The gipsies had

> "Folded their tents like the Arabs,
> And silently stole away."

A NEW DIDDLE.

SUCCESSFUL FOR A TIME, BUT "CAGED" AT LAST—A TAILOR TWICE SOLD—INTERESTING DETAILS, ETC.

A GERMAN, apparently about fifty years of age, dark features, short in stature, prepossessing in appearance, and of pleasing address, called on a certain day at a well-known tailoring establishment in New York city, and asked to see the proprietor of the place. When the proprietor made his appearance, the visitor, with sadness and utter despair pictured on his countenance, commenced to narrate a most doleful story as to how he had just arrived in this country from Europe, the barren condition of his once well-filled purse, the dreadful life he had led on the tempestuous seas, the loss of his dear sister and the idol of his heart during the trip, and now, without friends and without money, he was in a strange land. What to do he knew not. At this period of the sad tale he gave one long sigh, and taking out his handkerchief applied it to his eyes. Ah! this was too much for our tailoring friend—he had feelings, and this last sympathetic act had touched them, and at once caused him to manifest an interest in the stranger's welfare.

"My good man," said the kind-hearted knight of the needle, "I am sorry for you; your story is a sad one. I can only give you my mite, and wish I could afford more; it will at all events help you along."

To this the stranger indignantly replies, looking up from his handkerchief, "No, sir; I am too proud to accept of alms without giving an equivalent in return; but what I propose to do is, to show you what I discovered this morning while searching my poor sister's effects (weeping again); they are some things which she purchased in the old country, and have them here with me in this carpet-bag; and, sir, I am determined to sacrifice them all so as to procure enough to take me back to the land of my birth, where I have never known want. I hate to part with them, but my wants know no bounds, and they must be satisfied before this night closes. The things cost my poor sister $300 in gold, and we got them in without paying duty on them."

Just as the last part of the foregoing sentence was being completed, two nicely-dressed young men, of foreign nativity, came sauntering in the store with an air of purchase, and inquired the various prices for making different styles of clothing, what such a suit would be worth off of this or that piece of goods, etc., and while strolling around their eyes alighted on the goods of our destitute German, which consisted of handkerchiefs, table cloths, napkins, etc. Taking up some of the same and examining them, they remarked, "What are these handkerchiefs worth?" To which the proprietor replied that he was just about purchasing them. This caused a more careful examination on the part of the new comers, and in the meantime the story of the poor man is related to them.

"Well," says one of the young men, "I think I know dry goods when I see them—quality I mean—and will give $125 for the lot, and take my risks on the profits. What say you?"

"No," says the seller, "I am dealing with the proprietor only."

This, of course, ended the conversation on that topic, except, as the young men were going out, one of them remarked that if they were not sold, (pointing to the goods,) that he would take them at $125. His room was No. 106 Fifth Avenue Hotel, not to be later than five P. M., as they had to leave the city in an evening train; further, that when they visited the city again they would call at the tailoring establishment and purchase two suits of clothing.

After they had gone, the proprietor (having the "points" from two such apparently thoroughly "posted" men) was now more anxious to purchase than ever; money he loved, and he thought he saw a clear profit of $150 on the goods; the stranger wanted money, and now was his chance to make the purchase; so he offered $75 dollars for a starter. Then, after much talk, it got up to $150. The bargain was finally closed, the sum counted out and handed over to the stranger, who pocketed the same. After which, with uplifted hands, and a God bless you, concluding with a promise to return in the morning, so as to make the tailor a present of a small piece of silk with which to have a dress made for his child, in return for his kindness, the stranger made his exit, and the tailor returned to his counting-room, seated himself, and rubbed his hands together in high glee over his morning's work.

Time passed on, and by chance a friend of the tailor's

called in, who was a dealer in the goods which the tailor had just purchased.

"Well," said he, "what is that lot worth?" pointing to the recent purchase.

"Why, about $35. If you gave more, you are sold as well as the goods. The goods are of a common quality, all starched up, etc."

And sure enough, they were not worth over the price named by the gentleman.

At the announcement the tailor became indignant, swore revenge, and at once visited the Detective Police Agency, told his story, when the sequel was laughingly given by the Superintendent, as follows: That the two young men alluded to above were what are termed "coppers;" the destitute German, the "confidence operator;" and the tailor—an honest, confiding man—was the "out and injured" victim.

AN "ALL-RIGHT" DIDDLER.

The Steamer *Financier*, which used to ply between Cincinnati and Pittsburgh, had one day commenced her up trip, and had progressed to the point where the colored gentleman with the bell summons the "passengers to the Cap'n's office to settle." All complied with the urgent invitation, but one brawny Hoosier-looking chap, who took no notice of the summons, whatever, but walked the deck as important and consequential as if he owned the *Financier* and several other steamboats, and had a lease of the river they navigated, besides being owner of several large plantations they were passing. The clerk, who saw him so unheedful of the special call thus made, and supposing the man was resting under some misapprehension, approached him and asked him for his fare. The passenger looked at him as if half inclined to be offended, and responded, "All right!" in a tone which implied that he was perfectly at home, and had a full right there.

The clerk looked at him a moment: "Well," said he, "it may be all right; but it would be more right still if you would just fork over the money for your passage."

"All right," replied the Hoosier, nodding his head.

"Give me your fare," said the clerk, growing warm; "and stop your nonsense."

"All right," responded the man, waiving his hand.

"Oh, confound your 'all right,'" said the incensed clerk; "I say it isn't all right. I want the money, and I'll have it."

"All right," persisted the strange individual.

The clerk was almost frantic; but being called away to perform some other duties, the man was forgotten until they had passed the next landing place, when the clerk again demanded his fare, and again received the answer of "all right."

"Come, come," said the clerk, "shell out."

"All right," replied the incorrigible, as calm as a morning in May.

"Give me the money," yelled the clerk.

"All right," responded the man, showing not the least emotion; and to every demand or threat the reply still was, "All right."

At last the clerk, aggravated beyond all bounds, sought the captain, and informed him of the customer on deck, who, though strenuously persisting that all was right, to his mind, was all wrong, and asked his superior to look after him.

The captain went on deck, and with a frowning brow demanded the money.

"All right," said the man with the utmost gravity.

The captain stamped and swore terribly, but the man was not to be moved by such petty gusts, and the captain left him, vowing terrible vengeance when they shall reach the next landing place, which was Maysville.

As soon as the boat touched the wharf, the captain collared the delinquent; dragging him forcibly to the gangway, he ordered him to go ashore, with a voice of thunder, and assisted his departure by a process of ejectment not recognized in the courts, at the same time applying to him sundry strong words that profane men will sometimes use, to the horror of well-disposed people.

After the boat had swung from the wharf, the captain looked over the gunwale and deridingly asked his late customer if he would not like to go a little farther; and expressed the hope that he'd have a good time, and that he'd find it "all right" where he was, over the left!

The man heard him out, very complacently, when, applying his thumb to his nose, and describing certain mystical gyrations with his four outspread fingers, he cried, in a tone that drowned the noise of the steam, "All right, capt'ing! This is my hum, this is! I live in Maysville! All right!"

And the captain saw him walk leisurely up the landing, turning round occasionally and performing the same mystical signs, and fancied he heard the sound "All right!" borne toward him on the breeze.

FURNITURE DIDDLER.

A HOUSEKEEPER in want of a sofa is seen to go in and out of several cabinet warehouses. At length she arrives at one offering an excellent variety. She is accosted and invited to enter, by a polite and voluble individual at the door. She finds a sofa well adapted to her views, and, upon inquiring the price, is surprised and delighted to hear a sum named, at least twenty per cent. lower than her expectations. She hastens to make the purchase, gets a bill and receipt, leaves her address, with a request that the article be sent home as speedily as possible, and retires amid a profusion of bows from the storekeeper. The night arrives, and no sofa. The next day passes and still none. A servant is sent to make inquiry about the delay. The whole transaction is denied. No sofa has been sold, no money received—except by the diddler who played shopkeeper for the nonce.

Our cabinet warehouses are left entirely unattended, and thus afford every facility for a trick of this kind. Visitors enter, look at furniture, and depart unheeded and unseen. Should any one wish to purchase, or to inquire the price of an article, a bell is at hand, and this is considered amply sufficient..

FREE AND EASY DIDDLER.

A WELL-DRESSED individual enters a shop, makes a purchase to the value of a dollar, finds, much to his vexation, that he has left his pocket-book in another coat pocket, and so says to the shopkeeper :

"My dear sir, never mind; just oblige me, will you, by sending the bundle home? But stay; I really believe that I have nothing less than a five dollar bill, even there. However, you can send four dollars in change with the bundle, you know."

"Very good, sir," replies the shopkeeper, who entertains at once a lofty opinion of the highmindedness of his customer. "I know fellows," he says to himself, who would just have put the goods under their arm, and walked off with a promise to call and pay the dollar as they came by in the afternoon.

A boy is sent with the parcel and change. On the route, quite accidentally, he is met by the purchaser, who exclaims:

"Ah! this is my bundle, I see—I thought you had been home with it long ago. Well, go on! My wife, Mrs. Trotter, will give you the five dollars—I left instructions with her to that effect. The change you might as well give to me—I shall want some silver for the post office. Very good! One, two—is this a good quarter?—three, four—quite right! Say to Mrs. Trotter that you met me, and be sure now and do not loiter on the way."

The boy doesn't loiter at all, but he is a long time in getting back from his errand—for no lady of the precise name of Mrs. Trotter is to be discovered. He consoles himself, however, that he has not been such a fool as to leave the goods without the money, and re-entering his shop with a self-satisfied air, feels sensibly hurt and indignant when his master asks him what has become of the change.

A FEMALE DIDDLER

WRITES THREATENING LETTERS TO HER LANDLORD.

Not long ago, at St. Louis, a woman of many aliases was arrested on a charge of attempted robbery. This woman rented a small house of one Jacobs. She had not been long in the house before she discovered that it was sadly in need of repairs, and sent for the landlord to induce him to have the necessary work done. Jacobs, it seems, did not see it in that light, and thought the house was good enough. She then commenced writing letters to Jacobs, informing him that she had broken her leg by falling down the dilapidated stairs, and went so far as to have a suit brought against him for $10,000 damages. Not content with this, she continued writing to Jacobs, and threatened that, if he failed to make a certain arrangement with her lawyer, she would make a charge against him of violating her person. In some of her letters she uses words that no well-bred lady would employ in any emergency.

Jacobs, like a sensible man, instead of acceding to her demands, carefully preserved her letters, and finally had her arrested for attempted robbery. Being unable to procure bail, the woman was sent to jail. The following, one of the shortest of the letters, is published as a sample of the woman's style:

August 20, 1867.

A. S. Jacobs: Now, sir, your infamy shall be shown up, and I will sink you so deep in the fires of hell that you will not hear the last trumpet. You will be committed to the penitentiary for the rape you committed on me. We have all the proofs, and you shall be examined, and the . . . . . proven in court and to your wife. If you think you will escape me you are mistaken. I will go myself to her and tell her of your infamy. You see I am not alone and unprotected. If you do not do as the lawyer wishes you to, you shall have a hell on this earth. You thought you would have the rent raised up, but I will put you through, you old villain. She will make a nice hell for you, which shall be for life."

St. Louis boasted of several cases similar to this, in which unprincipled females have extorted money from respectable citizens by threatening to accuse them of immoral practices. In one case a woman obtained $5,000 from a wealthy citizen by the black mail process. In another, a notorious married woman and her husband extorted from a citizen a note for $4,000. It is said that a female who has a few respectable associates, has acquired property valued at $40,000 by similar arts.

DIDDLER IN THE SHINGLE BUSINESS.

A very gentlemanly man went into a store in Newburgh, N. Y., and with a business-like air priced various articles, stating casually that he lived about five miles from the city, and had a load of shingles which he intended taking home, but which were first to be loaded, and he had stepped in to buy his goods, and have them in readiness when the load was on. He was waited upon by one of the firm, and ordered quite a large bill of goods. While they were being put up, he drew a twenty dollar bill from his pocket, and asked the clerk to give him smaller bills for it. He held the twenty dollar bill in his hand until ten dollars had been counted out, when he took the money up, and asked him to give him sixty-five cents to pay a boy he had hired, and charge the whole amount with the groceries, saying he would be in as soon as he had "loaded his shingles" and liquidate.

The change was handed to him, and he stepped out of the door. It is thought he is experiencing considerable difficulty in getting his "shingles loaded," as, at last accounts, he has failed to make an appearance. No one recognized him, and it is to be presumed he is a professional traveling upon his wits.

YANKEE DOODLE DIDDLE.

Years ago, and now for aught we know, Yankee clock pedlars would go through the Southern States swindling and tricking the inhabitants most unmercifully. The following is a truthful instance:

One of those chevaliers took with him, in a long, Connecticut covered wagon, forty clocks, and sold and "put 'em up" along the country, in one direction, warranting them to keep "first-rate time." He exhausted his supply, with but a single exception, and then, with unparalleled assurance, he turned about and retraced his course. The last person to whom he had sold a clock hailed him as he was going by.

"Look o' here, stranger, that clock you sold me ain't worth a continental cuss. 'Twon't go at all!"

"You don't say so! Then, *you* must ha' got it, Square. See, the fact is, I find by my numbers that there was *one* o' my clocks—I had forty on 'um when I fust sot out—that I am a leetle afraid on; it was condemned to hum 'fore I came away, but some how or 'nother it got put into the wagon. What's the number o' your clock, Square?"

"Fourteen thousand and one," replied his victim.

"That's jist the blasted thing!" exclaimed the pedlar. "I'll change with yeou; yeou take my last one, and I'll take this hum. The *works* is good, I guess; on'y want fixin' a leetle."

The exchange was made, and all along the road the pedlar was similarly arrested by his dupes, who were similarly duped in return. He took every successive bad clock to his next customer, and received another bad clock for the next. And this was mentioned and laughed at as "Yankee cuteness." It strikes us forcibly, however, that swindling of the meanest kind would be a more appropriate designation for such a transaction.

CONFIDENCE IN CANADA.

MR. DIDDLER SETS OUT TO REVOLUTIONIZE THE BUSINESS OF MINING IN THE DOMINION AND GETS INTO TROUBLE.

An unpretending "shingle," denoting that a new corporation, yclept the "Julla Gold Mining Company," had been ushered into existence in Toronto. Neither the announcement nor the promoter of the undertaking caused a revolution in financial affairs, and the management and existence of the romantically named mine might have remained in oblivion but for the subsequent career of its promoter, a man who, during the three weeks of its career in that city, played as many sharp tricks as could be expected of the most expert adept in the same time.

Prior, however, to the transactions which summarily hastened the villain's "visit" to the county jail, was the initiation of a "mining company" advertisement for mineral lands in Madoc, announcing himself as an experienced miner desirous of purchasing, with a view of forming a company. Several answers appear to have been received, among these one from a party of gentlemen represented by Mr. Hugh Miller. With the latter he made terms, leasing, at a liberal sum, and for the term of twenty years, fifteen acres of lot No. 28, in the fourth concession of Madoc. The lease was drawn out to "Edward Pearse Pugh," the name given by the adroit rascal, but under the representation that he was the representative of an unlimited amount of American capital, ready to be flooded into the gold mining business as soon as the transfer was made.

As a first payment on the purchase, he offered a check for £100, with a signature purporting to be that of his father to Brown, Shipley & Co., of New York. This Mr. Miller hesitated to accept; but, in the mean time, proceeded to have the lease prepared, while "Pugh" forwarded the draft to New York. While the visions of nuggets from Madoc were thus to feast the imaginations of large investors in mining lands, the proprietor of the scheme proceeded to put the machinery in order, by which dividends of one thousand per cent. a week on the capital were to be obtained. A "preliminary" prospectus was issued, detailing the subterranean wonders existing in the auriferous region to become the property of the company as soon as the cash was secured.

The names of well-known citizens figured in this laudatory circular, and a happy time was promised for the Jullian venture.

An announcement intimated that shares were in readiness, but was evidently intended to strengthen public confidence in Pugh, who, on the latter day, visited a number of business men and made purchases on the strength of his position as secretary and manager of the company. His mode of operation displayed considerable genius, and would undoubtedly have been quite successful had he had less competent hands to watch him. After banking hours he visited a number of storekeepers, making purchases ranging from $30 to $100, in each instance giving checks for the amount, alleging that the banks being closed he could not draw money that day. To facilitate his game he wrote a letter on the same day to the Royal Canadian Bank, stating that a deposit of $12,000 to the credit of the Julla Gold Mining Company would be made on Monday.

With these arrangements completed, he visited the store of Mr. Potter, optician, and bought a theodolite, at $125, giving in payment a check for $140, and obtaining $15 in return to square the transaction. To Mr. Phillips, carver and gilder, he gave a check for $18 50, and at Wharin's he invested in a watch and chain at $50, paying the same worthless paper. At Ellis's jewelry store he purchased a like amount; at Morphy's $20 worth; with Mr. Booth, painter, he invested $12 50, serving each in the same way—giving checks over the sums owing and obtaining from them the balance in cash. Similarly assiduous, while the Saturday evening offered opportunities for work, he bought a gun from

Mr. Marston, and a revolver at a heavy price, a watch from Mr. Segsworth, jeweler, and, not to be without any of the requisites of a gentleman, bartered another check with Mr. Spooner for cigars, a handsome meerschaum, a cigar case, and other valuable articles.

At last he visited Merrick Bros., and made extensive purchases, proffering a similar barter; but they, hesitating, dispatched a messenger to one of the bank officials to ascertain the standing of Pugh, who with them had assumed the name of "H. S. Eccles." The report was unfovorable, and the matter being noised about, Mr. Potter also obtained information to a similar effect, and gave notice to the police. A detective was immediately on the track of the fellow; and, although receiving the information only about nine o'clock P. M., secured traces that led him to suspect his intention of leaving by the night train. Visiting the hotels, he found him leaving the Rochester House, to take the midnight train for Detroit. He was immediately arrested and depleted summarily of his heterogeneous assortment. While being taken to the police station, he made a determined attempt to escape, and succeeded in removing the grasp of the officer, but was recaptured.

On his person were found a number of documents which prove him to be a villain of no mean pretensions. Papers announcing him as the proprietor of a huge scheme called the "Cincinnati Financial and Discounting Association" were found on his person, and in this he occupied all the berths worth having. The affair is of quite recent origin, the prospectus bearing the date 27th of May, 1867. It was to have had a capital to the modest amount of $500,000. Any number of pawnbrokers' tickets disclosed one of his means of disposing of previous gains in the same way in Detroit and Cincinnati, while blank checks of French and English banks, English bill stamps, and other accessories, showed the variety of ways in which his roguery was prepared to show itself.

The "company's" check book, and other books and documents were found in the office, while in his pocket-book was found a list of tailors and clothiers to whom he had given orders for clothing, and some whom he had victimized. His stock in this line, had he secured all, would have consisted of four dress, seven tweed, and three overcoats, besides a case full of other clothing. A number of lesser transactions remain unrecorded, from the fact that sufficient are given to show the swindler one of the cleverest and most daring operators who has visited that city for some years. He is an Irishman, and states himself that he has not been long in America. He is well informed in regard to the country, however, and is a man of decided intelligence.

OFFICIAL DIDDLER.

The captain of a ship which is about to sail is presented by an official-looking person with an unusually moderate bill of city charges. Glad to get off so easily, and confused by a hundred duties pressing upon him all at once, he discharges the claim forthwith. In about fifteen minutes, another and less reasonable bill is handed him by one who soon makes it evident that the first collector was a diddler, and the original collection a diddle.

POCKET-BOOK DIDDLER.

A STEAMBOAT is casting loose from the wharf. A traveler, portmanteau in hand, is discovered running toward the wharf at full speed. Suddenly he makes a dead halt, stoops, and picks up something from the ground, in a very agitated manner. It is a pocket-book, and—

"Has any gentleman lost a pocket-book?" he cries.

No one can say that he has exactly lost a pocket-book; but a great excitement ensues, when the treasure trove is found to be of value. The boat, however, must not be detained.

"Time and tide wait for no man," says the captain.

"For God's sake, stay only a few minutes," says the finder of the book—"the claimant will presently appear."

"Can't wait," replies the man in authority; "cast off there, d'ye hear?"

"What am I to do?" asks the finder, in great tribulation. "I am about to leave the country for some years, and I cannot conscientiously retain this large amount in my possession. I beg pardon, sir," (here he addresses a gentleman on shore), "but you have the air of an honest man. Will you confer upon me the favor of taking charge of this pocket-book—I know I can trust you—and of advertising it? The notes, you see, amount to a very considerable sum. The owner will, no doubt, insist on rewarding you for your trouble"—

"*Me!*—no, *you!*—it was *you* who found the book."

"Well, if you *must* have it so—*I* will take a small reward—just to satisfy your scruples. Let me see —

why these notes are all hundreds—bless my soul! A hundred is too much to take—fifty would be quite enough, I am sure"—

"Cast off there!" says the captain.

"But then I have no change for a hundred, and upon the whole *you* had better"—

"Cast off there," says the captain.

"Never mind!" cries the gentleman on shore, who has been examining his pocket-book for the last minute or so—"never mind! *I* can fix it—here is a fifty on the Bank of North America—throw me the book."

And the over-conscientious finder takes the fifty with marked reluctance, and throws the gentleman the book, as desired, while the steamboat fumes and fizzes on her way. In about half an hour after her departure the "large amount" is seen to be a "counterfeit presentment" and the whole thing a diddle.

NEW JERSEY MULE DRIVER.

HOW MULES ARE DRIVEN, AND HOW A VETERAN DRIVER EVADED A GATE-KEEPER—A JERSEY REMINISCENCE.

ALMOST every one is familiar with the mode of driving (?) a drove of young mules. It is on the inverse system. The drover buys up from fifty to a hundred young, unbroken mules, and mounted on a brood mare, they follow after the same as do sheep the bell-wether of a flock. For a great many years an old trader, familiarly called "Old Sol"—who if ever possessed of any other patrynomic had probably forgotten the fact—was in the habit of bringing in from the West a drove of the long-eared animals and disposing of them to the farmers of south Jersey. The last business visit he made to that section was about the time the turnpike mania raged, and a single bar was stretched across nearly every public road, to pass beyond which required the payment of:

For every carriage, sleigh or sled drawn by one beast, $1\frac{1}{2}$ cents per mile.

For every additional beast, $1\frac{1}{2}$ cents.

For every dozen of calves, sheep or hogs, 2 cents.

For every dozen horses, mules or cattle, 6 cents.

"Old Sol" had passed something like two dozen of these bars on his way from Camden to Bridgeton, paying the legal exaction at each under protest, and in very profane language. Not having disposed of a single mule, and drawing nigh the end of a long journey, he was beginning to suffer from a drought in his pocket, and to his dismay saw the inevitable bar once more before him. Looking around, and finding that his mules were leisurely browsing along the road, some two or three hundred yards behind, he hurried up his pace to the gate, paid a single toll for the horse he was riding, and made a special request of the gate-keeper to shut it after him, and stop those darned mules which had been following him two or three miles.

"Certainly," said the accommodating keeper, who had it locked in less time than it takes to tell it.

"Old Sol" started off again on a brisk canter, which his mules soon imitated, and as they came to the gate bar went over it in one, two, three order, to the astonishment of the keeper, who saw the point of the joke in a few minutes after, and acknowledged himself "dead beat."

BEWARE OF THE WIDOWS.

A YOUNG PITTSBURGH WIDOW DIDDLES A CLEVELANDER.

THE reporter of the Cleveland *Herald* has a young friend who came to Pittsburgh, and was victimized by a gushing young widow at a hotel there to the tune of $430. The reporter tells the story thus:

It seems that he went to Pittsburgh on a visit, and while there at the hotel he made the acquaintance of a pretty young widow, who had just escaped the "weeds" the first day of his acquaintance, and appeared at the dinner table arrayed in an elegant light silk, and, as he states, looked charming, all smiles and geniality. This table acquaintance ripened into a sofa tête-a-tête, and long lingering walks in the evening, stopping now and then to "cream and soda," and an intimacy that could not be misunderstood by the landlady of the hotel. So finding that their actions were watched, she entreated him to leave her; but that was just the "game" to make him stay by her side, as he did, much to the displeasure of the landlady, who took no pains to hide this ill-feeling from the parties.

In order to escape these persecutions, as she termed the actions of the landlady, she proposed a trip to Cincinnati and Louisville, and our friend, having but little to occupy his time, consented, and away they went as fast as express trains could carry them.

They remained in these cities for a few weeks, and growing tired of the dull sameness of city life, (there were no first-class amusements to be attained,) concluded to try a few weeks on the lake shore, in the

THE PITTSBURGH WIDOW.

Forest City. They arrived on the morning express, and took lodgings at a first-class boarding-house up town.

During this acquaintance our friend had trusted considerable sums of money to the charming widow for safe keeping, he being nervous about pocket-picking and burglary, and when they arrived here she had about $430 in her possession which belonged to him. The day previous to his telling us of his loss, business called him to Oberlin, Ohio, where he was obliged to remain one night.

Upon his return to this city in the morning, his first thought was for the widow—of the pleasure it would give him to meet her again, after an absence of twenty hours—and he had provided a very fine bouquet for the occasion, to convince the dear creature that with him at least it was not "out of sight, out of mind." The swiftest horses were employed to convey him from the depot to the house containing his adored. Arrived at the house, he rushed, school-boy fashion, up the steps, through the hall, up another flight of stairs, and into her room, to find her—gone, and his $430 with her.

He met the landlady on the stairs as he came down, who, in answer to his inquiries, said that the lady had packed her trunks and left the house about an hour after him on the day before, and that she said she was going into the country to rusticate until her *husband* returned!

Our friend paid the bills and left the house, a wiser if not a richer man. As he is one of Fortune's favorites, the loss of the money don't trouble him; but, as he expresses it, "that he should be bamboozled by a dashing widow!"

HOW A PHILADELPHIA POLICEMAN

GOT DIDDLED BY A WIDOW IN TEARS.

A WOMAN, genteelly dressed, called at the Mayor's office in Philadelphia, and appeared to be in deep distress, so much so that she shed tears quite freely, and a suit of deep mourning served to add to the effect produced. She represented that she had been to Washington, to get the body of her dear deceased husband, and that her port-monnaie, containing all the money she had, was stolen in one of the cars on Pennsylvania Avenue. She further represented that she was a resident of New York State, whither she was going, but could not go on without some assistance, to enable her to pay railroad fare, etc. She had, however, a money order on the National Bank at Jervisport, N. Y., which if she could get cashed would place her in funds.

On its face the order seemed to be for $90 50, and Officer Reeder accompanied her to a broker's office on Third street, to see if it could be paid there, or, if not, whether an advance could not be obtained upon it. As the woman was unknown, and could not get any one to vouch for her character, the broker refused to either cash the order or advance any money upon it.

Policeman Reeder, then, in consideration of the woman's situation, advanced $15 to her, the money order being retained as security for the advance.

In due time the order was sent to the bank at Jervisport, through the broker referred to, and instead of $90 50 being returned, there came back but $9 50. The order had been so skillfully altered that it escaped detection, until it reached the officers of the Jervisport Bank.

The woman in black has not been heard from since. The policeman is out of pocket $5 50, unless the widow returns and makes it up.

A VERY CLEVER SWINDLE BY A PAIR OF DIDDLERS.

A DISINTERESTED STAKEHOLDER HAS HIS OPTICS CLOSED BY "SHOWERS OF THE QUEER."

At Detroit, an old man from the East, who refused to give his name, was swindled out of $40 in the most approved style. He was standing on the sidewalk in front of the Russell House, when two strangers came along disputing as to the result of one of the base ball games. They talked in an angry tone as they drew near him, and finally one of them offered to bet $15 that he was right, and proposed to put the stakes in the old man's hands, while they went up stairs to find out who was right.

The old man took the money, two $20 bills, and the sharpers went up stairs, leaving it in his hands. Shortly afterward they returned, one of them acknowledging he was beaten, and demanded the stakes, which were immediately given up to the winner. The proper change could not be made by the fortunate winner, and he asked the old man to keep the two twenties and give him small bills for them. He did so, and the two left, after thanking him for his kindness in acting as stakeholder, also for his honesty in not leaving while they were gone, and treated him to a drink. Shortly afterward he had occasion to pay out some money, and presented one of his $20 bills in payment for several small articles he had purchased. It was immediately pronounced a counterfeit, and an examination of the other bill revealed the fact that it was worthless.

The old gentleman took his loss with the greatest coolness, and made no complaint to the police, although, as he himself says, he thought he was a d—euced sight smarter than he had shown himself. He, fortunately, has plenty of money, and will not be discommoded by the loss.

A BOGUS DETECTIVE VICTIMIZES A LIQUOR DEALER.

A WELL-DRESSED fellow, with a companion, found his way into a bar-room in a certain city, which was not effectually closed, and, after obtaining a glass of wine, he informed the proprietor of the place that he was a New York detective, and that it was his duty to arrest him for violating the Excise law.

At this juncture, the companion alluded to suggested a compromise. The "detective" and liquor dealer assented. Ten dollars was thought sufficient by the liquor dealer; but the "detective" became indignant when offered so small a sum. He finally accepted $50.

RUM-DIDDLE-DUM.

ON a winter night, I was riding through the little town of Lowell, Maine. My route lay along upon a high ridge of land between the Cold Stream Pond and the Passadumkeag Stream. The large full moon was just rising in the horizon, looking larger than ever. The sleighing was excellent, and my horse, as if charmed by the scene, was trotting off at a brisk rate, when, from some cause, he suddenly stopped. On looking for it, I discovered a horse and sleigh, driverless. In the sleigh was a mysterious-looking keg, sole master of the premises; and upon looking for the driver, I found that individual by the roadside. The keg was evidently master of him as of the sleigh. He was muttering something to himself about a "thundering cold fire," and blaming an imaginary John for not "putting on more wood!" On going nearer to him, I found that he was sitting upon the snow, his feet through the fence, *warming them at the moon!*

NO SECOND DIDDLE FOR PAT.

"A BRIGHT mornin' to your fair face, Mistress Murphy."

"Well, a good morning, Pat."

"Och, Mistress Murphy, whiniver I see a rale shiny, Irish mornin' like this, it puts me in mind of the ould country, and of the time whin I lived wid yer father—rest his sowl. A dacenter man niver drew breath, and sorra a poor craythe niver passed his door without a bit or a sup."

"Troth he was, Pat."

"Mistress Murphy," pulling a flask out of his pocket, "would ye thrust me for a half-pint till I go down to the wharf, and may —— fly away wid the roof of my jacket but I'll pay ye before the sun goes to bed?"

"Burn the dhrap, Pat, till ye pay for the half-pint ye got yesterday."

"Mistress Murphy," said Pat, emphatically, "I knew yer mother, and she was an ould hod-carrier, 'un yer father was a dirty washerwoman, an' I seed him hauled with six roarin' big bulls to the gallows, ye ould, ugly——"

Pat sloped in double-quick time, with a pewter-mug at his heels.

A VERY MEAN DIDDLER.

A CONFIDENCE OPERATOR ARRESTED.

As Detective Thompson, of the Twenty-seventh Precinct, New York city, was patrolling through West street, he noticed Charles Smith, a notorious pocket-book dropper and confidence operator, on the lookout for a victim. Soon William Burgard, a newly-landed emigrant, who had arrived at this port on the Northern Light, came along, and Smith followed him closely, and suddenly dropped a package made up to resemble gold coin and greenbacks, close to Burgard's heels. This, of course, attracted the stranger's attention, and, as he turned about, Smith informed him that he had just found a package containing a large sum of money, and, as it was contrary to law to retain anything found in that manner, he proposed to sell the package to Burgard.

The emigrant swallowed the bait so artfully held out by the confidence operator, and followed him to a secluded spot on Pier 10, North River, where he handed Smith four $20 gold pieces and three $10 Treasury notes, in exchange for which he received the package in possession of the confidence man, and which was found to consist of a patent medicine advertisement and two notes for "$100" each on the "Bank of Free Love, in the State of Matrimony." These proceedings had been closely watched by the detective, who, when the bargain had been consummated, stepped in and arrested the operator, and found the victim's money in his possession. Smith was arraigned before Justice Hogan at the Tombs and committed for trial. He is a native of Germany, thirty years of age. He has been a very successful operator, and victimized a great many emigrants and countrymen.

MR. JEREMIAH DIDDLER.

THAT WELL-KNOWN GENTLEMAN ON HIS TRAVELS—HE PERFORMS AN OPERATION IN TROY, BUT DRAWS IT MILDER THAN HE MIGHT HAVE DONE.

A genteel and well-dressed man, representing in all respects the character of a merchant which he assumed, called at the shirt and collar establishment of Messrs. S. A. House & Sons, Troy, and walking up to the senior partner, addressed him very familiarly with the salutation, "Why, how do you do, Mr. House?" Mr. House did not remember the stranger, at which the latter expressed great surprise, saying that he was formerly connected with a prominent establishment in New York, and had purchased at different times large amounts of goods of him, and recalled names and facts with such truthfulness that Mr. House inwardly inveighed against a "shocking bad memory," while he was gradually preparing to accept as gospel truth all the fellow said to him.

After some conversation, Mr. H. inquired what his visitor was doing now, and was informed that he was a partner in a newly established house in the metropolis, naming the firm, and would look over his stock of goods, with an eye to purchase a limited quantity. The goods were, of course, displayed, and the sharper picked out a quantity amounting in the aggregate to $250. He desired thirty days' time. "Are you reported?" inquired Mr. House. "Oh, certainly, sir," said the buyer, and upon examining the register, Mr. H. found that the firm named by the sharper was set down as A No. 1. Of course the time was readily granted, and in the presence of the stranger the goods were packed and directed to the New York establishment. Suddenly, as if recollecting himself, the stranger remarked that after all he thought he would not want time upon the goods—he had a check for three hundred dollars in his pocket, which he should not require, and if Mr. H. would give him the balance, he would pay for the goods at once.

The check was drawn in the name of the firm, and Mr. House paid over the balance of $50, with which the operator departed, enjoining Mr. H. to ship the goods at once to New York. The goods were sent, and the check was deposited in the bank for collection. In a day or two a letter was received from the New York firm by the Messrs. House, to the effect that a quantity of goods had been received by them which had not been ordered, and desiring to be informed of the circumstances. The next day brought a letter in regard to the check. That, too, had been received; it was a forgery.

If Mr. House had not previously suspected from the tenor of the first letter that he had been victimized, he was now positively assured of it; but as the firm which had received the goods very generously offered to accept them, he will not in any event be a loser to the extent of more than the $50 balance between the bill and the forged check. The operation was very ingeniously conceived, and most adroitly executed. After the fellow demonstated his status so finely, it is not too much to say that he might have victimized even the sagacious House to a much larger extent than he did.

DIDDLER PLAYS A SHARP GAME

AT PHILADELPHIA.

A MAN, said to be red-faced, red-whiskered, and pursy, with the air of a grandee, went to Philadelphia, and obtained the services of about fifty Germans—who were far from being in even moderate circumstances, and then out of work—to pluck peaches for him in his extensive orchards near Delaware City. Only too rejoiced to get something to do, these fifty Germans gave their assent, and, headed by their new-found employer, entered the railroad depot, from which they were to take the train for Delaware City.

Before entering the cars, our large-faced but small-hearted man went to each of his employes and collected $1 16 to pay their fare as a party, he averred. This sum each gave willingly out of their magic purses, which they hoped to well replenish soon; and this individual received about $65 in all.

The train started with the party, and when about five miles out the conductor came for his fare. The Germans referred him to their employer; but he, to their great astonishment, was nowhere to be found. The whole party were put off the train, and after waiting long and anxiously for their quondam friend and supposed benefactor, who never came, the truth burst upon them that they had been swindled out of what little they possessed, and were many miles away from their homes, with the darkness of night all around them.

A PETTY DIDDLER.

A WELL-DRESSED man called at the furniture store of E. Minzesheimer, No. 877 Sixth Avenue, New York city, and purchased a chair for $2 50, for which he tendered a $50 bill in payment. The person in charge of the store did not have sufficient change for the bill. The man then told him to send the chair to No. 18 East Forty-ninth street. The chair was accordingly sent to the place indicated, but nobody there knew anything about it, and the boy returned to the store.

Soon after the man came into the store again and told the person in charge that the lady had returned home, and the chair should be sent to the house again with sufficient change for a $20 bill. The lad started with the chair and $17 50 in change, and when near the house he was met by the man, who relieved him of the chair and money, and gave him nothing in return, and then decamped.

SILVER COIN DIDDLER.

HE PLAYS THE MYSTERIOUS DREAM DODGE ON A HOSPITABLE FARMER.

A STRANGER once stopped at a farm-house in Paris, Ohio, and asked permission to stay over night, which was readily granted by the hospitable farmer. A couple of hours after retiring for the night, the stranger was taken suddenly and violently ill, and for several days was apparently deranged.

On his recovery he informed his host that during his illness he had dreamed three nights in succession that he had discovered, in a certain ravine near the house, under a rock, an earthen crock containing a large amount of silver. At this the old gentleman expressed surprise, and spoke of it as being a very mysterious dream. Afterward, however, they were walking together in that direction, and the dream was again adverted to by the stranger. An examination was at once proposed by the farmer, to satisfy their curiosity.

The rock was soon found, and after brushing the leaves carefully away, it was removed, and, to their utter amazement, there set a crock full of silver. They took it out and conveyed it secretly to the house, and on examination it was found to contain four hundred dollars, all in half dollars, which they agreed to divide equally between them.

The day after this discovery, as the stranger was about to take his leave, he complained to his benefactor of the inconvenience of carrying so much silver, when an exchange was proposed, the stranger receiving two hundred and fifty dollars in greenbacks for his share of the coin, silver then being at a premium of about fifty per cent.

It was not long after the departure of his guest, however, till mine host made another discovery—his four hundred dollars in silver were counterfeit! and he had thus been ingeniously swindled out of two hundred and fifty dollars. The story was kept quiet for several months, but it finally leaked out.

A BOLD DIDDLER.

A CAMP meeting, or something similar, is to be held at a certain spot which is accessible only by means of a free bridge. A diddler stations himself upon this bridge, respectfully informs all passers by of the new county law, which establishes a toll of one cent for foot passengers, two for horses and donkeys, and so forth, and so forth. Some grumble, but all submit, and the diddler goes home a wealthier man by some fifty or sixty dollars well earned. This taking a toll from a great crowd of people is an exceedingly troublesome thing.

A DIDDLER AND HIS DOG.

A FRIEND holds one of the diddler's promises to pay, filled up and signed in due form, upon the ordinary blanks printed in red ink. The diddler purchases one or two dozen of these blanks, and every day dips one of them in his soup, makes his dog jump for it, and finally gives it to him as a *bonne bouche.* The note arriving at maturity, the diddler, with the diddler's dog, calls upon the friend, and the promise to pay is made the topic of discussion. The friend produces it from his *escritoire*, and is in the act of reaching it to the diddler, when up jumps the diddler's dog and devours it forthwith. The diddler is not only surprised but vexed and incensed at the absurd behavior of his dog, and expresses his entire readiness to cancel the obligation at any moment when the evidence of the obligation shall be forthcoming.

A VERY MINUTE DIDDLE.

A LADY is insulted in the street by a diddler's accomplice. The diddler himself flies to her assistance, and, giving his friend a comfortable thrashing, insists upon attending the lady to her own door. He bows, with his hand upon his heart, and most respectfully bids her adieu. She entreats him, as her deliverer, to walk in and be introduced to her brother and papa. With a sigh, he declines to do so.

"Is there *no* way, then, sir," she murmurs, "in which I may be permitted to testify my gratitude?"

"Why, yes, madam, there is. Will you be kind enough to lend me a couple of shillings?"

In the first excitement of the moment the lady decides upon fainting outright. Upon second thought, however, she opens her purse strings and delivers the specie.

Now, this, I say, is a minute diddle—for one entire moiety of the sum borrowed has to be paid to the gentleman who had the trouble of performing the insult, and who had then to stand still and be thrashed for performing it.

A COOL PHILOSOPHER.

A young scamp, boarding at one of the hotels, in San Francisco, had managed for a long time, by one artifice or another, to postpone the payment of his bill. At last the landlord became quite impatient, and stepping up to his boarder, slapping him gently on the shoulder, asked him for some money.

"I have not a red cent about me at present," was the laconic reply.

"But, my dear sir," said the landlord, "I cannot afford to keep a boarding-house without being paid."

"Well, sir," exclaimed the young philosopher, "if you cannot afford it, sell out to some one who can."

AN UNSUCCESSFUL DIDDLER IN BOSTON.

Recently a man named Alfred Watson, thirty-eight years of age, was arrested in the Campbell House, Wilson's lane, on the charge of forging the names of four or five firms in Boston, to checks for different amounts, and obtaining goods to the amount of $2,773 75 on the spurious paper, all of which (principally sewing silks) has been recovered.

Watson was arrested, and hails from St. Louis. He brought one colored man with him, and hired another for the day immediately after his arrival there. His mode of obtaining goods, it seems, was to visit a store and lay out a bill of goods, saying he would call for them next day. Instead of calling himself, he sent the two colored men to the different places named, with a bogus note and check for each for the amount of the bill, in whatever name he might have made the purchase.

It is believed that every dollar's worth of property he obtained has been recovered. One of a firm whom he attempted to swindle had his suspicions excited when the colored man offered him the note containing the check, which he sent to Heyes Brothers & Co., to ascertain if it was genuine. As soon as the messenger left with the check, the colored man, being the one who came with Watson, took to his heels, and fled for the Campbell House, pursued by a clerk, but he effected his escape. The man hired there was locked up as a witness.

AN UPPER CRUST DIDDLER.

AN "ARTFUL DODGER" DODGES TO THE TUNE OF $10,000.

In the summer of 1867, Detective Vaughan, of New York city, was ordered to work up a case of horse stealing, which, for the audacity displayed by the thief, deserves special mention. A gay and stylish-looking young man, who gave his name as H. E. Adams, called at a livery stable, corner of Fourth-street and Lafayette Place, and engaged a light wagon and horse, which he ordered to be sent to the Spingler House, in Union Square, near Fourteenth-street. The proprietor was about to send the finest horse in his establishment at first, as he thought the young man would be better pleased by the attention thus paid him; but on second thoughts did not, but forwarded a very fine light carriage. When the stable man arrived at the Spingler House with the turn-out, he met Mr. "Adams" standing on the stoop, pulling on his kids. Evening came on, on Friday, but the Lafayette Place stable-keeper could not see anything of his horse and wagon. About ten o'clock in the evening, however, a stable-keeper in Seventy-first street, near Third avenue, arrived at the Lafayette Place establishment with the horse of the proprietor, which had been hired to the aristocratic "Adams." He said that "Adams" had called upon him and ordered him to give him a better horse, for which favor he would pay him his own price, and that he would add to his obligations did he take the Lafayette Place horse to his stables. The result of this neat manœuvre was, that "Adams" secured a splendid horse from one establishment, and as splendid a carriage from the other. Since this nice little game was played, Detective Vaughan has been looking for "Adams," and said "Adams" is not. It has been ascertained that the rascal has been carrying on this dodge for several years past, and it is alleged that his ill-gotten gains from its successful issue, amounts to $12,000.

A DIDDLER ON HIS TRAVELS.

HE FALLS IN LOVE WITH AN IOWA LADY, MARRIES HER, AND BRINGS UP IN JAIL.

An accomplished and beautiful young lady of Bellevue, Iowa, was married to a young man who was smitten by her charms as he saw her on the levee one day while the boat was passing. He learned her name and opened a correspondence with her, which resulted in marriage. What happened after that is told by the St. Louis "Democrat," as follows:

Frank Marsden, *alias* Morton, was arrested by officer Jaques, on a telegram received from Brick Pomeroy, of the La Cross "Democrat," offering a reward of $100 for his arrest. The man is charged with falsely representing himself as an authorized agent of the "Democrat," obtaining railroad passes as such, and other indiscretions.

The officer found Captain Marsden, as he styles himself, hard at work as an upholsterer, in the shop of F. Darke, on Olive-street, between Twelfth and Thirteenth. There is a touch of romance in the history of this man which shows that he has a taking way with the ladies as well as with newspaper editors. It is stated that some time ago, at Bellevue, Iowa, he saw some young ladies looking at a steamboat which was in the act of landing. He became interested with one of them, a beautiful and highly respectable girl of about seventeen years. He asked a gentleman to tell him the name of the fair girl, and having learned it, he sat down and wrote a letter to his charmer, full of protestations of love, and all that sort of nonsense. The girl read, believed, felt flattered, and a correspondence ensued, ending in an engagement of marriage. A short time after Marsden went up to Bellevue, married the imprudent young lady, and brought her to this city. The following night the young wife visited her husband at the station house, and wept bitterly on discovering the character of the man she had sworn to love through life. She happened to have friends in the city, and one of them took charge of her, and sent her back to her parents in Iowa. Romantic young ladies and school girls who delight in anonymous correspondence, should learn a lesson from the experience of this unfortunate young woman.

AN OLD GERMAN GENT

IS "DONE" OUT OF $250 BY HIS EMPLOYERS.

Two men, who gave their names as Saunders and Adams, rented the office No. 34 Pearl street, Buffalo, for the purpose, as they declared, of carrying on a real estate and insurance business, paying them the sum of $19 in advance. They furnished the office with five or six dollars' worth of chairs and other stuff, and advertised for a clerk who understood German. The advertisement was answered by an elderly gentleman of the Teutonic faith, and he was engaged at a stipulated salary, having first, in compliance with the demand of Messrs. Saunders & Adams, deposited with them the sum of $250 "as security." In pursuance of these arrangements, the elderly gentleman went down to the place of business on Tuesday morning last, and "opened the office." Business was not very good, and the clerk grew impatient at the non-appearance of his employers. They came not; they have not come yet; neither have they been heard from; and ye clerk mourneth the loss of his situation and his $250.

A SMALL, BUT SCIENTIFIC DIDDLE.

The diddler approaches the bar of a tavern, and demands a couple of twists of tobacco. These are handed to him, when, having slightly examined them, he says:

"I don't much like this tobacco. Here, take it back and give me a glass of brandy and water in its place."

The brandy and water is furnished and imbibed, and the diddler makes his way to the door ; but the voice of the tavern keeper arrests him.

"I believe, sir, you have forgotten to pay for your brandy and water."

"Pay for my brandy and water!—didn't I give you the tobacco for the brandy and water? What more would you have?"

"But, sir, if you please, I don't remember that you paid for the tobacco."

"What do you mean by that, you scoundrel? Didn't I give you back your tobacco? Isn't that your tobacco lying there? Do you expect me to pay for what I did not take?"

"But, sir," says the publican, now rather at a loss what to say, "but, sir"—

"But me no buts, sir," interrupts the diddler, apparently in very high dudgeon, and slamming the door after him as he makes his escape. "But me no buts, sir, and none of your tricks upon travelers."

A SHARP DIDDLER.

A PURSE or pocket-book being lost, the loser inserts in one of the daily papers of a large city a fully descriptive advertisement.

Whereupon our diddler copies the facts of the advertisement, with a change of heading, of general phraseology and address. The original, for instance, is long and verbose, is headed "A Pocket-book Lost," and requires the treasure when found, to be left at No. 1 Tom street. The copy is brief, and being headed with "Lost" only, indicates No. 2 Dick, or No. 3 Harry street, as the locality at which the owner may be seen. Moreover, it is inserted in at least five or six of the daily papers of the day, while in point of time it makes its appearance only a few hours after the original. Should it be read by the loser of the purse, he would hardly suspect it to have any reference to his own misfortune. But, of course, the chances are five or six to one, that the finder will repair to the address given by the diddler, rather than to that pointed out by the rightful proprietor. The former pays the reward, pockets the treasure and decamps.

DIAMOND DIDDLER.

A LADY of ton has dropped, somewhere in the street, a diamond ring of very unusual value. For its recovery, she offers some forty or fifty dollars reward—giving in her advertisement, a very minute description of the gem, and of its settings, and declaring that, upon its restoration to No. so and so, in such and such avenue, the reward will be paid *instanter*, without a single question being asked. During the lady's absence from home, a day or two afterward, a ring is heard at the door of No. so and so, in such and such avenue. A servant appears, the lady of the house is asked for and is declared to be out; at which astounding information the visitor expresses the most poignant regret. His business is of importance and concerns the lady herself. In fact, he had the good fortune to find her diamond ring. But, perhaps it would be as well that he should call again.

"By no means!" says the servant; and "By no means!" says the lady's sister and the lady's sister-in-law, who are summoned forthwith. The ring is clamorously identified, the reward is paid, and the finder is nearly thrust out of doors. The lady returns, and expresses some little dissatisfaction with her sister and sister-in-law, because they happen to have paid forty or fifty dollars for a fac-simile of her diamond ring—a fac-simile made out of real pinchbeck and unquestionable paste.

EVERY MAN, WOMAN AND CHILD

SHOULD READ "THE PAPERS," AND NOT RELY ALTOGETHER ON THE BIBLE FOR NEWS.

Daniel H. Miller, hailing from Waterford, Erie County, Penn., was swindled out of $225 in Detroit, by the check game. Miller had been up in Genesee County, where he had sold a parcel of land for $225, which he had sewed up in his vest. A man who had been traveling with him on the cars from the country, walked along with him toward the boat for Chicago, which Miller was to take passage on, and when near the boat they were met by another "gentleman," who asked Miller's companion for the money due on some goods. The other said he had nothing but a check for $2,500, and that was of no use until morning; but he thought Miller would oblige him with a loan of some money until then.

Miller unsuspectingly let the sharpers cut the money out of his vest, when the two operators went away, telling Miller to be at the bank to-morrow, in time to get his money. After a while Miller began to think that all was not right, and he informed an officer of the affair, who took him to the station, where he told his story, but he was unable to describe the men. He seemed utterly cast down, as it was all the money he had in the world, and he intended to buy him a few acres of land in Pennsylvania. When asked if he had read the newspapers, he said that he read nothing but the Bible, and the result is that he is $225 out.

HOW LORD THURLOW DIDDLED

A HORSE DEALER.

WHEN Thurlow began his legal career, he was at his wits' end to procure a horse, without which he could not have gone on circuit. He had obtained his wig and other paraphernalia on "tick," but how was he to get credit from that peculiarly sharp specimen of British merchants, the horse-dealer? By dint of impudence and cleverness he succeeded. Entering the yard of one of the species, he called in authoritative tones for "a very superior roadster." The price was no consideration. "Show me a horse that you can recommend, and if I like him after trial, I'll have him at your own price." The bold, imperious manner of the young scamp imposed an the tradesman; a strong and serviceable hackney was saddled; the young barrister was mounted, and forthwith rode off on circuit to Winchester. Before the owner saw the steed again, it had carried the impudent and unscrupulous young lawyer to every town on the western circuit. It can excite no surprise, though it reflects lasting infamy on the hero of the story, to learn that the delivery of the horse was accompanied with a note from Thurlow to the effect that "the animal, notwithstanding some good points, did not altogether suit him."

DIDDLER IN THE COAL BUSINESS.

A GENTLEMAN in Thirteenth-street, New York city, was waited upon by an individual who represented that he had two tuns of coal aboard of a vessel, and, having no use for it, was anxious to dispose of it at $4 a tun. The gentleman consented to the purchase, and in the afternoon a tun reached the residence. The individual was on hand, and when the coal was put in, demanded $4 of the occupant, which amount was paid to him. Later in the day another tun arrived, and with it came a bill for two tuns of coal purchased from a coal-yard in the vicinity. The buyer set about making an investigation, and to his astonishment, found that he had been victimized. The swindler had ordered the coal from a neighboring yard, and had given instructions to send it to such a residence.

DIDDLER IN THE SHOE BUSINESS.

ONE OF THE LATEST TRICKS.

THE ingenuity of the thieving or diddling fraternity would almost seem to be inexhaustible, for scarcely a week passes without the reading public being startled or amused by the revelation of some new dodge to circumvent the law of *meum et tuum*. A Bolton, Mass., shoe dealer was made the victim of a most daring and yet a somewhat ingenious trick. A tall man, having the appearance of a member of one of the building trades, entered his shop, and desired to be shown a pair of shoes of the best quality. A pair was at once submitted to his inspection, but they were pronounced to be not quite good enough. He wanted a pair of the best quality the tradesman had in his shop; the price was not of the slightest consequence. A pair was next reached from the shelf, which the tradesman pronounced to be equal to any that could be purchased in Bolton; the price was twenty-four shillings.

The man tried them on, and found them to be, as he expressed it, "just the ticket;" therefore he would become the purchaser, keep them on his feet and leave the old "leathers" to be repaired.

Whilst the tradesman was on his knees feeling at the new shoes, and satisfying himself that the fit was admirable, a fellow who had been loafing about the door for some minutes rushed into the shop, and at one blow knocked the customer to the floor.

The tradesman was almost panic-stricken; but the man who had been knocked down jumped to his feet instanter, and started in pursuit of his assailant, who was tearing away at a rapid rate across the market square.

"My word," exclaimed the shoe dealer, as he rushed to the door to witness the chase, "but if he catches yon ruffian he'll make him hutch."

The two men soon disappeared down Oxford street, and they may be running yet for ought that is known to the contrary. Certain it is that the shoe dealer has never seen one or the other since, nor the color of his money.

HOW HE DONE THE TAILOR.

"WILL you pay this bill, sir?" said a tailor to a diddling fellow, who owed him a pretty long bill.

"Do you owe anybody anything?" said he.

"No, sir," said the tailor.

"Then, you can afford to wait;" and off walked the tailor.

A day or two afterwards the tailor called again.

Diddler was not at his wit's end yet. So, turning to his creditor, he said:

"Are you in debt to anybody?"

"Yes, sir," said the tailor.

"Why don't you pay?"

"I've not the money."

"That's just my case, sir. I am glad to see that you appreciate my condition; give us your hand!"

A SMALL DIDDLER,

MADE SUNDRY PURCHASES AND BORROWED A TRIFLING SUM OF MONEY.

A VERDANT-LOOKING man entered a grocery store in Hartford, Conn., and wanted to make sundry purchases. He was very particular as to the quality of everything.

"Have you got any molasses, Mr. Keeney?—not molasses I don't mean—syrup, sir, syrup?"

Mr. Keeney had got just that, and the man took a gallon—and bought a jug to put it in.

"Any extra mackerel, Mr. Keeney?—something very nice I want."

He was supplied with what he wanted, and then continued his inquiries for this thing and that, until he had run up a bill of about $35.

About this time a lad entered the store, somewhat in a hurry, and approaching the stranger, had a moment's private conversation with him, when the latter was seen to take a roll of bills out of his pocket.

"I declare," said he, "I haven't got it, but hold on a minute!"

At this he went up to Mr. Keeney and said:

"See here, my wife has sent up my boy to get $9 35, with which she wants to pay a dry goods bill down town. I haven't got anything less than a $20; suppose you let the boy have the amount, and put it in with my bill, and I'll pay it all at once."

Mr. Keeney had no objection to this arrangement, and so he gave the boy $9 35, who immediately started off to reach his mother.

"There, by thunder!" ejaculated the rural purchaser just as the lad departed, "I've forgot one thing; have you got any kerosene?"

"Yes."

"Is it first-rate?"

"It is."

"Well, I'll take a gallon. I brought a can along to get it in, and I'll go and get it in the wagon."

And he started, since which time he has not been seen in the vicinity of Mr. Keeney's store.

A PREACHER SWINDLED BY A LOTTERY.

A PREACHER who lives in a distant State, and whose cupidity appears to have got the better of his judgment, writes the following account of the way in which he was swindled by some sharpers having an office in this city. No doubt, there are hundreds of similar cases, and we print this as a warning to persons who may be tempted in a like manner.

He says that last summer a New York firm sent out an advertisement of a gift enterprise that appeared on its face so just and honorable an undertaking that he was induced to send them ten dollars for eleven tickets. The tickets were received, and soon after the men sent him eight more, requesting him to distribute them. His family took five, and three of his neighbors took the others. They next sent sixteen more tickets, which the minister returned.

In a short time the sixteen tickets were sent back by the lottery men, with the offer that if the minister would pay for them, and did not draw a valuable prize, they would make him a handsome present. This bait took, and ten dollars were paid for them. Another sixteen tickets were finally sent to this greenhorn, who was told that they were the last, as the million and a half of tickets had been sold. If ten dollars were sent to the lottery-men they guaranteed the minister a prize worth two hundred dollars at the grand drawing, which was to take place on the 24th of October.

The money was sent, and the various sums were acknowledged. Early in November, the minister received a letter saying that one of his tickets had drawn a prize worth two hundred dollars, but that they levied five per cent. on the prizes, and that ten dollars more must be sent on before the prize would be forwarded. This ten dollars was also sent, but was never acknowledged, and the minister heard nothing more from his friends.

He now expresses a desire to come to New York, and prosecute them, but his journey would prove fruitless. He has learned a lesson which may be worth the money it cost him. At all events, it ought to prove a warning to others. If any one offers a gold watch worth one hundred dollars for two or ten dollars, he is a cheat, and ought to be avoided as much as a pickpocket.

DIDDLING A LAWYER.

THE CLIENT MORE CUNNING THAN THE COUNSEL.

The shrewdest men are sometimes taken in by the cunning scoundrels who travel about the country and live by swindling the credulous. Even lawyers, who know a thief by the expression of his eye, are sometimes victimized by their clients. One of these criminal lawyers, while canvassing the St. Louis jail in search of a client, came across a fellow whose case was hopeless. The prisoner engaged the lawyer to defend him, and when questioned about the fee, said he had no money with him, but had $500 in his trunk, which was at a farm house about ten miles in the country. He gave the lawyer an order for the trunk, and the learned counsel loaned his client $10 or $15 for present use.

The lawyer then hired a buggy, and went into the country after the trunk with the $500 in it. He could not find the house, and returned to the city, feeling very bad. Calling at the jail he told his client that he had deceived him, but the prisoner insisted that the lawyer had taken the wrong road, and gave such minute directions about finding the house, that the lawyer was convinced of his sincerity, and after making another small advance to his client, went out again to find the valuable trunk. He failed again to find the house, and was now thoroughly satisfied that he had been victimized. On seeing the prisoner again, the rogue laughed at him, and told him he did not think he was so green. The only satisfaction the attorney had was in seeing the thief sent to the penitentiary.

DIDDLER BROTHERS.

A COUNTRY GENTLEMAN FALLS IN WITH THE NEPHEW OF A GOVERNOR AND A CONNECTION OF THE ROTHSCHILDS—AN EXCHANGE OF GOOD GREENBACKS FOR BAD GOLD.

IN Rochester, New York, an illustrious scion of a noble ancestry, by name at least, rejoicing in the appellation of Nimrod Buckingham, a distant relative of the duke, as well as an heir of Anneke Jans, hailing from Middletown, Dauphin County, Penn., was "honswoggled" out of $108 by a nephew of Gov. Geary, of Pennsylvania, and his partner in the lumber business, who was a connection of one of the Rothschilds, of Europe, and minister apparent to Sitka, with an eye also to the ice trade. Nimrod had cut his eye-teeth. He had traveled and read the Middletown newspapers and a patent medicine almanac. He fell in with the two distinguished gentlemen above mentioned on the train from Canada West, at Suspension Bridge, by overhearing Gov. Geary's nephew ask the descendant of the Rothschild if he had sold his lumber. To which he replied in the affirmative, and at good prices.

"How much did you get?" says Geary.

"Fifteen thousand dollars," says Sitka.

"Where is it to be delivered?"

"At Rochester," says Sitka.

At which Nimrod, of Buckingham, who was from a lumber as well as a coal country, chimed in. At first the distinguished gentlemen were a little reserved and shy of the stranger, but as he appeared to be an honest sort of fellow, their reserve wore away, and before reaching Rochester, the trio were on pretty good terms, and Buckingham was a "hunky boy."

On approaching Rochester, Sitka had to meet a man at Congress Hall, and pay him for the transportation of his lumber. Unfortunately, all his money was in gold, and he appealed to Geary for greenbacks; but Geary was in the same fix. It was really too bad, and there was no exchange office near the depot. What should they do? Here the noble Buckingham came to the rescue, and with an eye to making a piece, he volunteered to let Sitka have $108 in greenbacks for the four $20 gold pieces he had in his hands—an exchange Sitka thanked him for.

The bright dreams of Buckingham came to an end when he found that he had been taken in and regularly done for. He appealed to the police, but the train was gone, and carried with it his brilliant friends and his hard-earned stamps. His gold he can keep as a relic of bygone days, or sell it for old brass. In the meantime, he declares that when he travels again he will buy his tickets through, and have the "old woman" sew his money in his pantaloons, so that to obtain it will require a man strong enough to lift him out of a "cheer."

NOT TO BE DIDDLED.

ARMING WAITERS WITH FAMILY SYRINGES IN ORDER TO PREVENT FRAUDS.

Bonifaces are more subject to imposition from penniless travelers than any other class of purveyors, and it must be admitted, also meet with less sympathy when they are taken in. If what we hear of Vallejo landlords be true, they must have suffered a heap of martyrdom from itinerant Bohemians before they resorted to their present ingenious measure of self-defense. It seems that the rule adopted there is to pay for dinner immediately upon the delivery of the plate of soup. A fraudulent genius, after having unsuccessfully exploited one hotel, boldly entered the Hashington and called for dinner. He was astonished to see the waiter approach him with a plate of soup in one hand, a towel in the other, and a large family syringe under his arm. The waiter laid the plate of soup in front of the customer, and significantly placed the palm of his right hand under the nose of the hungry customer. As our friend had not as yet tackled his meal, he modestly inquired the meaning of the open hand.

"Pay in advance," was the terse and peremptory reply of the waiter.

"Can't you wait till I get through my meal first?"

"No, sir. Our rules are positive. On delivery of the soup plunge down the cash."

"Singular promptitude," he muttered. Then reddening up with natural indignation, said he,

"I suppose if I don't pay you, you'll brain me with that bludgeon pump of yours?"

"Not at all, sir. Through this instrument we secure our business on a cash basis. Your money, if you please!"

He thought he had the dead-wood on the soup anyhow, and dipped his spoon for the first mouthful. Before the spoon reached the broth, however, he was transfixed at seeing the waiter coolly introduce the point of his syringe into the plate, and pulling the suction handle out to its fullest extent, the soup suddenly disappeared, leaving his plate as empty as his stomach. He turned around, but the waiter had passed to another customer, and our friend left the establishment in disgust.

HOW FIELDING DONE A JEW

OUT OF TEN GUINEAS.

The following anecdote is told of the celebrated Henry Fielding:

"The son of one Boaz de Paba, a celebrated Jew, was on the point of marrying a Christian lady. His father made no objection to the intended wife's religion, but was greatly dissatisfied with the match on account of her small fortune, in consequence of which he refused his consent. The son, who was desperately in love, threatened that he would marry her without his consent, and the father, in his turn, threatened that he would not give him a shilling. The young Jew answered that he would force him to do it; and that if he refused dividing his substance with him, he would get himself baptized, to enjoy the benefit of the English law, which (then) assigned to a Jew child becoming a Christian the half of the father's property. Boaz, confounded at this answer, went to consult Fielding, to know if such a law really existed. Fielding told him that it did exist, and was in full force; but added, if he would give him ten guineas, he would put him in a way of frustrating his son's hopes, so that he should not be able to get a farthing. Boaz instantly told down ten guineas. Fielding, having pocketed the money, told him that his only remedy was to "turn Christian himself.'"

A JEWELRY DIDDLER.

A CONFIDENCE man went to a jewelry store in Boston, and represented himself as a son of E. Benjamin, the New Haven, Ct., jeweler, bought $500 worth of diamonds, and had them sent to his "father" by express, C. O. D. He then told the man of whom he had made his purchase, that he wanted to buy some jewelry of another firm in the city, and asked him to go over and introduce him to the firm. Accordingly he was introduced as Benjamin's son, bought $400 worth of goods, and ordered them to be sent as the others were, but gave in payment a forged check on Benjamin for $500, and received $100 in good money as change. The goods were sent to their destination, but were repudiated and sent back by Benjamin, when the Boston man discovered that he had been cleverly swindled.

A COLORED DIDDLER.

A COUNTRY gentleman of color went to Lynchburg, Va., and sold a lot of tobacco to the amount of $25, when, being accosted by a town practitioner of the same color, he was informed that he must join "The League." He was also requested to entrust his new acquaintance with the money, who agreed to put it in the hands of "the general who would give him $60 in gold for it a month." He was tickled with this idea; gave up his greenbacks to the traveling depository, who has not since been heard of. The "stranger who was taken in" lodged a complaint with the police. Country darkeys should keep their eyes open when they come to town.

ANOTHER.

AN elderly colored man brought a basket of eggs and a lot of chickens to the Petersburgh market. While waiting for some purchaser for his little stock, another colored man came up to him and asked him to take charge of the three small water melons which he had. The old man from the country readily consented. Having occasion to leave his eggs and chickens, he asked the one whom he had found to watch his things until he came back, which he did in a few moments, but only to find "dat ar man" had made a swap, taking eggs and chickens away, and leaving in exchange the three pitiful melons.

A DIDDLE WITH A TAIL IN IT.

HOOKY WALKER, some years ago, visited Bridgeport, Conn., and pasted the dead walls of the place with the following announcement, in a poster, printed in brilliant colored inks:

THE WOOLLY HORSE OUTDONE!

EXHIBITION OF

A HORSE WITH A TAIL WHERE HIS HEAD SHOULD BE!!!

ALSO,

A HORSE WITH A HEAD WHERE THE TAIL SHOULD BE!!!

ADMITTANCE, 25 CENTS. CHILDREN, HALF PRICE.

COME ONE, COME ALL!

HARMONY HALL, MONDAY, 8TH INST., 7 O'CLOCK.

This advertisement was the talk of the citizens for several days before the opening of the exhibition. The hour at last arrived, and Harmony Hall was crowded to its utmost capacity. The entertainment commenced with a "concert" by a troupe of second-rate minstrels, concluding with a "plantation break-down."

Immediately after, the lights were lowered—a hint for the audience to disperse.

"But where is the curiosity—the horse advertised in the poster?" asked an inquisitive gentleman.

"Here, sir," said the showman. "Any person wishing to see the horse, come this way."

We followed diddler through a side-door into a stable, and there beheld *a horse with his tail in the manger!*

"You must admit, gentlemen, that his head ought to be where his tail is."

"That's so," said Pat Rooney, "for I niver saw an animal except an elephint swallow hay with his tail."

We acknowledged the "sell," and next day advised our acquaintances to patronize "the curiosity." In a few days we had many sympathizing friends in our misfortune.

Diddler hauled off soon after from Harmony Hall, with his pockets well lined with quarters.

A ROBBER DIDDLER.

In Cincinnati, a robber, of the Paul Clifford school, entered a boarding-house, and, nosing his way uninterrupted by any one to a room in the second story, occupied by a lady and gentleman, both of whom happened to be out, he made free with what came under his observation. He donned a fine overcoat belonging to the gentleman, and was about to investigate the drawers of the bureau, when he heard a noise upon the stairway, and he started for the door. There he was met by the lady occupant, who, in the politest manner imaginable, he saluted with:

"Ah! this is Mrs. B., I presume. Your husband sent me after his overcoat, as he is just about to start for St. Louis, and was so much engaged he had not time to come for it himself."

The lady, supposing him to be one of the attaches of the office in which her husband was engaged, and knowing that he was often called away at a moment's notice, simply remarked:

"All right, but won't he be up before he leaves?"

Receiving an answer in the negative, she said:

"Here, take this $20 note, and tell him to send me that package of Christmas presents I spoke to him about."

The fellow took the note and left, no doubt chuckling all over with the successful issue of his bold attempt.

A DUTCHMAN NOT TO BE DIDDLED.

A GENTLEMAN stepped into a Dutch grocery to get a $1 bill changed. The Dutchman had heard of $10 bills being altered from $1. He took the one offered him, and held it up to the light.

"What are you doing that for?" inquired the man.

His answer was brilliant.

"I wish to see if dish bill have been altered from a $10."

PRESIDENT JOHNSON GETS A SMALL BITE.

AN Englishman, representing himself as a delegate from the striking tailors in London, received $50 from President Johnson, to aid the knights of the needle who had been thrown out of employment by "strike." It now turns out that the man was an impostor.

GLASS DIDDLERS.

A WIDE-AWAKE scoundrel in Nashua, N. H., stumbled against a storekeeper's window and broke a large pane of glass. He then handed the keeper of the store a counterfeit $100 bill to pay the damages, and received back $90 in good money, with which he incontinently sloped.

A SOMEWHAT similar case happened in Newark, N. J., recently. A young man, apparently greatly intoxicated, made a sudden lurch against a store window, breaking a large pane of plate glass. In an instant the shopkeeper had him by the collar, demanding pay for the damage. The fellow protested, with many hiccups, that he had no money, when he was dragged into the store, where, in accordance with the advice of some of his neighbors, the storekeeper searched his prisoner. The search resulted in finding a $100 greenback in the fellow's pocket. This bill was immediately transferred to the money-drawer, from which the merchant drew two $20 bills, and handed them to his "victim," saying, "It will cost me just $60 to get that glass replaced. Here's your change, sir, and now be off, and keep whiskey out of your head in future. This will be a good lesson to you."

The fellow took the $40, and, placing it in his wallet, walked off, apparently considerably sobered by the transaction.

Soon after he had disappeared, the shopkeeper ascertained that the $100 greenback was a rank counterfeit.

TWO DIDDLERS VISIT NEW YORK.

THEY CUT WITH DIAMONDS.

Mr. Julius Silversmith Diddler, one of the real Simon-pure stock, possessing the genteel appearance and handsome countenance of the aristocratic Diddler family, accompanied by his friend, A. Cheat, Esq., of Coney Castle, L. I., (of course a lie,) dashingly drove up to the leading jewelry store on Broadway, New York city.

Alighting from one of Miner & Stevens's handsome barouches, they entered the store, and requested the clerk to show them some diamonds; and after examining several lots put before them, they selected a set of diamond ear-drops, a brooch, and ring, all solitaires, valued at $12,156.

"We have not the money handy, but you can drive with us to *our* residence in Fifth Avenue, where you can obtain payment for the diamonds."

"What name shall I enter in the order-book, gentlemen?" asked the clerk.

"Barnum Brothers," replied Diddler.

"Wait a moment, and I will accompany you," said the clerk, after consulting with one of the firm.

Putting on his hat and coat, the clerk jumped into the barouche, and the customers drove up to *their* residence.

"Where is the governor?" inquired Diddler of the servant in attendance. "I want—"

"Brother," said the other Diddler, immediately interrupting him, "go out to the 'building,' and see him there."

The "brother" went out, and shortly after returned with a check on a city bank for $12,156, purporting to be signed by James W. Barnum and certified.

The clerk pocketed the check, handed Diddler the diamonds, and started for his employers' store.

As a matter of course the check was presented at the bank soon afterwards, the firm desiring to be satisfied that it was good; but the bank didn't know anything about Mr. Barnum, nor any bank account of his, so the firm "smelled a mice," and wisely came to the conclusion that they had been swindled; but who were the swindlers and how they came to live in a respectable house on Fifth Avenue were questions which it was all very well to ask, but which were not easily answered.

To the house on Fifth Avenue, therefore, did one of the firm go, but, alas! the birds had flown, and the only information he could obtain was, that the same day the diamonds were purchased the two gentlemen had hired apartments in the house at $100 a week, giving as their reference a city banker; but the latter gentleman knew nothing about the fellows it appears.

Diddler likes cutting (away) with diamonds.

AN EDITOR DIDDLED.

Some time ago, an editor of a popular weekly magazine in Boston came to New York city on business, and while passing through Chatham street, a mock auction store attracted his attention. A thought struck him (a pity it had not knocked him over)—"I will beard the lion in his den," he being of course already posted in their manner of doing business.

He *went in*, and bought a genuine gold watch for a hundred and some odd dollars; he *came out* with a pinch-beck, worth about a dollar and a half!

"What shall I do?" thought he, "as I now perceive that I have been made an ass. To expose the transaction to the police, the reporters will get hold of it, and make a laughing-stock of me. I will keep quiet."

And so he did for a while, but he finally "let the cat out of the bag," by communicating the transaction to some confidential friends. Of course they kept the secret, over the left, and soon after the affair was published all over the country.

We advise all, and especially editors and ministers, to keep out of mock-auction stores, gift enterprises, and all other rat-traps that may be met with in almost every street in the city.

The Postmaster has lent his aid towards breaking up the gift enterprise business. He proposes to cut them off from the facilities of the mail, and to test the case he has seized upon a large number of letters addressed to these concerns, and holds them subject to the advice or action of the Attorney General, who has been notified of the frauding. Complaints are made daily to the Mayor or Justices by parties who have been swindled by these gift concerns, which take all sorts of shapes, frequently borrowing the mantle of charity or patriotism as a disguise.

They are generally so managed that after the victim has parted with his money he has no remedy at law; the transaction is covered in such a way as to evade the law against swindling and false pretences, though it is a swindle of the most barefaced kind. It is a cunningly-devised trap into which people will walk with their eyes wide open. There are plenty of gullible people in the city, but the country is the safest field for the operations of these sharpers. Circulars are sent to all the country towns and villages to persons whose names and addresses are collected by their agents for the purpose. One of the most successful dodges is to inform the parties addressed that they have drawn a valuable prize in some scheme, which will be sent to them on remittance of a few dollars. The gudgeon takes the bait, forwards the money, and either hears no more about it, or gets in return a piece of brass jewelry, or some other worthless article.

If these swindlers can be shut off from the privileges of the mail, their business will be effectually broken up. It is to be hoped, therefore, that the Attorney General may be able to find authority in the law for sustaining the action of the Postmaster.

THE GREAT

GETTYSBURGH ENTERPRISE SWINDLE.

The men who get up these enterprises have sheltered themselves of late under the pretence of aiding patriotic or charitable undertakings, and in the name of Soldiers' Hospitals and Orphan Asylums have frequently succeeded in their schemes.

The most pretentious of these swindles was the Gettysburgh Asylum Lottery, which the Attorney-General of Pennsylvania had the courage to denounce, and he drove its headquarters from Philadelphia to New York. The scheme was so plausible that the Secretary of the Treasury was imposed upon and remitted the Government tax on lotteries for its benefit.

General Van Wyck took the matter up in Congress, exposed the fraudulent misrepresentations of the prospectus of the concern, and moved a Committee of Inquiry into the action of the Secretary of the Treasury in remitting the tax, which has led to a full investigation and exposure of the swindle.

The following is the report of the Congressional Committee:

"The Committee on Retrenchment, to whom was referred the report of the Commissioner of Internal Revenue, giving the reasons why the scheme known as the Gettysburgh Asylum for Invalid Soldiers, was exempt from the payment of special tax, would report:

"That they examined many witnesses, among them

some of the originators of the scheme, and interested in its success; and the prominent facts were obtained from its friends and not its enemies. Substantially the facts are as follows: Before the close of the war, a prominent and wealthy tobacconist of New York city, Mr. John Anderson, for greater security, invested largely in diamonds, paying for the same, as was claimed, between one hundred and fifty and two hundred thousand dollars. A portion thereof, and the last lot obtained, were in some particulars tainted with fraud. Criminal proceedings were instituted by Mr. Anderson and his friends. So great was the crime, and so clear the proof, that the swindlers were arrested. No other diamonds but these are advertised in the Gettysburgh lottery.

"After the war government bonds advanced, while diamonds purchased with gold at 200 and 280 rapidly declined. Mr. Anderson wanted to realize on his diamonds, and also expressed a desire to aid disabled soldiers; both objects commendable if pursued in an upright and legal manner. After due deliberation by some friends, gathered at Mr. Anderson's house, among them one or more prominent gentlemen from the State of Pennsylvania, an enterprise to establish an asylum at Gettysburgh was agreed upon, and at the outset the nature of the scheme is manifested by the character and the men obtained to carry out the design. Experts of large experience in that which was to be its leading feature, and who were valuable by reason of their knowledge of the devices whereby the laws against gambling could be evaded, the credulous entrapped, the moralist and Christian assured that vice was only an exterior under cover of which piety and charity might be fully developed, were required, and R. France, P. A. Edgerton, and S. T. Dickinson, well known as professional lottery gamblers, were selected, as leaders, in a cause, the only ostensible object of which was to benefit disabled soldiers. As the sentiment of the Christian world, and particularly the laws of New York, were opposed to all species of gambling, these men immediately take counsel how the moral sense can be deceived and the laws defied.

"They appeal to an eminent lawyer, one who had long been their counsel, ex-Recorder Smith, and he informed them that the courts in the case of art union associations had decided against all lotteries, no matter what the object, or however cunningly devised; and that an act of the Legislature would not afford the pretext they sought, because the constitution of that State forbids the Legislature from legalizing any lotteries.

"They then wished him to examine the constitutions of all the States to ascertain one, if possible, where no prohibition existed, so they could make an attempt for incorporation. Judge Smith pursued the inquiry, and in due time reported that the State of Pennsylvania had no such prohibition. Thither these charitable patriots directed their steps, and hid away from public gaze they pull the wires, and moving in the shadow of the names of Generals Meade and Pennypacker as incorporators and trustees, with the promise of $300,000 to the treasury of that State, procure a charter, masking the real design under the clause authorizing fairs. The act nowhere justifying a lottery such as they advertised.

"Ten thousand dollars advanced by Mr. Anderson were paid into the treasury of Pennsylvania. A meeting of the trustees was called. Neither Generals Meade or Pennypacker were present, and only one of the trustees in the bill. The mask is now removed. A resolution passed making France, Edgerton, and Dickinson, members of the association. The master spirits step upon the boards. Another resolution is passed making them supervisors of the asylum. The charter provided that before each *disposition* of property $10,000 should be paid into the treasury. This contemplated thirty different *dispositions*. The programme was then arranged to draw $400,000 from the people before each disposition; making $12,000,000 to be collected, at least $6,000,000 of which would go to the operators.

"After opposition appeared in Pennsylvania these shrewd men discover they could not have more than one *disposition*, and as they were only required to pay $10,000 before each disposition, without regard to the amount of money raised, or value of property disposed, they determine to raise $1,200,000 before the first disposition.

"The legal trustees met. They refused to ratify the proceedings of the former meeting. General Meade requested the opinion of the Attorney-General of the State, which was in denunciation of the project, and all who participated therein were liable to indictment, when General Meade pronounced it a swindle, he and Pennypacker withdrawing.

"Strange, then, that men whose only object was charity should run the hazard of the law's punishment; not strange that France, Edgerton, and Dickinson should, for they had often taken such chances.

"It has been asked why Mr. Anderson, who had entire control of the scheme, should not have then withdrawn his aid. He was afraid of his diamonds, then on exhibition in Philadelphia, lest they might be seized by the police, and removed them to New York city. Here more devices were required to protect them from an anticipated raid by the police of that city. Mature deliberation was again had, and it was concluded to exhibit the jewels at one place, while the office of the operators should be at another. Then, if the police came to make an arrest, and should seize, as they were by law required, everything connected with the crime, and on exhibition, that they would, however, not be justified in seizing articles in another building.

"After the charter was obtained, making up the prizes involved some discussion. Mr. Anderson first proposed to enter one thousand acres of oil land he owned in Pennsylvania, but, as petroleum was at a discount, it was thought diamonds would be more attractive, and as he alleged he had paid over $150,000 for them, and been at some expense, he was to receive, cost and expenses, nearly $200,000, yet they were valued in the scheme at $300,000. Mr. Anderson knew that $100,000 were to be realized by some parties, yet suffers the fraud to go on unrebuked.

"Then Judge Smith, whose legal advice had been valuable, was offered an opportunity to show his sympathy for the disabled soldier, and he offers a farm in Sullivan county, with some valuable stock, which he valued to the managers at $45,000, while they withhold the stock and present the farm at $60,000. Here some one was to be enriched by the value of the stock and $15,000; yet the Judge takes no exception. When an expose is made, and the managers find they must go to the wall on the farm, they prudently withdraw it, but too late to remove the character of the operation.

"The testimony shows that at a forced sale the farm

might bring $6,000; a very liberal estimate would be from $8,000 to $10,000; while on the assessor's book of the town it is valued at $3,500. The fact of withdrawal is a concession of the fraud.

"A portion of the diamonds of Mr. Anderson claimed to have been a swindle upon him, and can be none the less so on the public. Some of the diamonds are said to be couplets; that is, a genuine top on an inferior bottom, difficult of detection after setting. On many of them Mr. Anderson had advanced money as a loan, yet so inferior were they by reason of size and quality, although genuine diamonds, that they were not redeemed. The owners, having played a sharp game, never intended to redeem them.

"In the list is the yacht Henrietta, proven to be probably worth $20,000, valued by the managers at $50,000. The managers in this case have no doubt increased the valuation given by her owner.

"Mr. Anderson called on Mr. Jones, publisher of the New York *Times*, who was interested in the publication of the Tribute Book, many of which remained unsold, as it had no value for general reading, its main attraction being some plates and elegant binding; 1,000 copies were offered at $20 each; then Mr. Jones solicited newspapers to make no attack upon the scheme.

"Not satisfied with the indorsement of the Pennsylvania Legislature, they seek to defraud the revenue from the payment of tax, knowing that such exemption will be considered an additional guarantee of the good faith of the project. They made application to John H. Deihl, Collector of the Second District of Pennsylvania, May 28, 1867. He knew that the good faith of the transaction was questioned; that the Attorney-

General of his State had denounced it; that General Meade had withdrawn from and denounced it; if he ascertained the facts, which the discharge of his duties required, he knew their character did not authorize the scheme they were projecting. He knew from their charter that only $10,000 were to be appropriated to the object of the charity previous to each drawing, and that by their by-laws passed March 14, 1864, all moneys realized after paying the $10,000 were to be retained by France & Co., yet Mr. Deihl certifies 'all the net proceeds were to be appropriated to the object of the charity.'

"Mr. Diehl states in his certificate that Attorney-General Brewster had brought the case before the Supreme Court. He also adds that three eminent counsel, naming them, had given an opinion affirming its legality, whereas one of them, Mr. Meredith, has published a letter denying that he ever gave any such opinion. Mr. Deihl may have supposed it to be all right, or he would probably not have allowed his son to be appointed receiver for the concern.

"The Postmaster-General, who had advised all postmasters to aid this 'truly patriotic and benevolent enterprise,' found that he had been deceived, and by his authority the editor of the *Mail*, in the December number, says: 'We are authorized by the Postmaster-General to say, that at the time he was induced to sign this recommendation he believed the enterprise was a praiseworthy one, and intended to aid a noble charity; but that he has become convinced that the scheme has been perverted to fraudulent purposes, and he desires to withdraw the recommendation he then made.'

"This scheme uses the pretext of benefit to disabled

soldiers. In their name we protest against the prostitution of sympathy for the scars and empty sleeves, and holy impulses of charity for their misfortunes to furnish a market for certain property, at fictitious values and large profits to men, whether of acknowledged wealth and social position, or needy adventurers and professed gamblers.

"After the difficulty in Pennsylvania, France & Co. were elbowed out of the ground, as alleged by one witness, that their character as lottery-men was injuring the concern; yet that character was the only consideration for their employment, and Mr. Hitchcock, who had been successful in a previous gift enterprise, substituted. After ten months' operation, the proof is that not sufficient money has yet been realized to meet expenses. The prospect of any drawing is very remote. Mr. Hitchcock testified that the expenses were about $80,000 more than the receipts, only $20,000 having been received. He also established that some of the trustees met at Philadelphia, on the 10th January, 1868, and passed a resolution that the net proceeds of the concern should be appropriated to the object of the charity.

"The passage of such resolution at so late a day can not relieve the scheme from the charges made, and, like the withdrawal of the farm, are certainly suspicious, if not conclusive evidence against it. At the same time a resolution was passed authorizing the President of the association to make a contract with Mr. Hitchcock for the management of the affairs, and that contract may be so made as to swallow up a portion of the whole profits. Lotteries and gambling of all kinds are condemned by well-regulated communities.

"Unfortunately, during the war, Congress sanctioned,

indirectly, lotteries for religious and charitable purposes, by exempting them from the payment of special tax; the object was to encourage every expedient to raise money for the soldiers. As that was a war measure, Congress should make haste to repeal it, particularly since it is now used to pander to the passion for gambling, and a means of profit to operators. There has not, probably, been since the war, a scheme of this kind of any proportions which was not commenced primarily and really to benefit the originators. All lotteries are swindles. Yet by far the most dangerous lotteries are those where vice is made attractive, where a sense of the crime is deadened, and consciousness of the guilt removed, by the pleasing delusion that honorable names endorse, and a pretended good end justify, violations of the law; yet there is not a tithe of the excuse there is for a man bankrupted by misfortune staking his last dollar upon a throw of the dice or a shuffle of the cards. There has been more demoralization in this country from gift enterprises than any other single cause. Not only all classes, but each sex and all ages are drawn into the giddy whirl, and many, in buying a first ticket here, will spend their last dollar at the gaming table. Already the harvest has been prolific in an outgrowth of villainous schemes, each with a different device, such as Elmore & Co., Clark, Webster & Co.; jewelry distribution; Toilet Watch Company; the Pen and Pencil; Kelly's Pictorial, and others, each with its own trick to victimize the ignorant and credulous.

A society of distinguished gentlemen, for the prevention of gambling, may be organized to hunt up the dens concealed from view, studiously avoiding public attention, where only now and then a victim is lured, but not guilty of the meanness of covering their crime under the guise of charity, and the mantle of religion. Yet hand-bills fill the city and adorn the press, telling where a large gambling house is in operation, and diamonds are publicly exposed to entrap and allure. What an ally to aid charity, to be used sometimes as a handmaid to religion! Would it be any more pernicious to allow professed gamblers to sit down in the vestry room, the session room, or the body of the church, and there with dice and cards and other paraphernalia of the gambling table, no more criminal than the wheel, if they donate a portion of their unholy gains to the benefit of the church? Yet, in some sections, moral men, professors of religion, ministers of the gospel, have interested themselves to popularize this vice by seeking aid through its influence.

The committee recommend the adoption of the following resolution:

Resolved, That the Commissioner of Internal Revenue be requested to revoke the permit heretofore given, exempting the Gettysburg Asylum for Disabled Soldiers from the payment of special tax and license, said revocation to take effect from May 28, 1867, and that taxes and license be collected from said association the same as if no permit had ever been given."

Love's Experiment.

Pretty Governess.—"How often must I tell you how to wear your hats? You are provokingly slow to learn! This is the third time to-day within an hour that I have placed your hats properly upon your heads. There!"

Children retire under their beavers, and the lovers improve the opportunity in practising certain labial mysteries known to the initiated.

HODGE-PODGE.

Did you ever go up to the printers,
And see all those devils at work?
I swagger, they beat all the flinters,
What fellows they are for a joke!

AN EGG DISASTER.

A MINISTER OF THE GOSPEL ATTEMPTS TO SPREAD HIMSELF—DEPLORABLE RESULT.

Among the goods expressed from the West by the D. & S. C. Railroad were a number of baskets of hen-fruit. Two or three stations this side of that at which they were placed upon the car, an ex-minister of huge proportions and of the gospel stepped into the express car, and our clerical friend accidentally took his position in front of them with his back behind him and toward the eggs. While the twain were conversing, the train started forward. The man of God was taken unawares by the unexpected jerk, and lost his balance. He found it in the basket of eggs just in his rear. He also found his rear in the basket of eggs.

The result of this ministerial onset—if we may so term it—baffles description. Of course the contents of the basket came to an unlucky end. His profession prohibited profanity in the presence of a fellow-traveler to eternity; yet his theological tenets did not incline him to albuminous immersion, and he was conscious of no disease that required a mucilaginous sitz-bath. Ike Partington once set a hen on fifty-two eggs, just to see her spread herself; here was a man not used to the business, who had set himself on fifty-two dozen, and successfully accomplished the same result, as any one could see. But though backward in getting into this undignified position, he was by no means backward in getting out. He erected himself and examined himself. Any member of his church, if present, would have recognized in him not only a faithful fellow-laborer, but an earnest yolk-fellow.

For about a minute he stood motionless, except as he, with spread and tremulous fingers, in an undecided and uncertain way, waved his hands about the seat of war, with the air of a man who had been egged on to desperation. He certainly presented a ludicrous aspect. As the precious ointment ran down Aaron's beard, so the albuminous unguent ran down the preacher's trowser's legs, spreading in translucent liquidness upon the floor about his feet till he looked like a school-boy who had been injudiciously deprived of recess. The express messenger took the stove hearth and did what he could toward cleaning off his friend—a novel way of "scraping an acquaintance." Hesitating to return to the passenger car lest he might present a butt for the ridicule of the ungodly and the scoffer, he sat down upon a box near the stove, and by the time he reached Dubuque was pretty dry—so dry that when he attempted to leave the car he at once fell upon his knees on the depot platform—not in prayer or thanksgiving, as spectators naturally at first supposed, but because the stiffness of his clothing rendered it impossible for him to straighten up.

THE *N. Y. Tribune* seldom indulges in a joke, but when it does, why, "there's something in it," as may be seen by the following:

"T—— bought a gallon of Otard at Brady's to take home, and by the way of a label, wrote his name upon a card, which happened to be the seven of clubs, and tied it to the handle. Alderman C—— coming along and observing the jug, remarked, 'That's an awful careless way to leave that liquor.' 'Why so,' said Tom. 'Why? because somebody might come along with the eight spot and take it!'"

SHERIDAN, by his extravagances, run himself over head and ears in debt, and seeming very little concerned about it, one of his friends told him one day that he wondered how he could sleep quietly in his bed whilst he was so much in debt. "For my part," said Sheridan, "I sleep very well; but I wonder how my creditors can."

"JOHN PAUL" says: "Amid all the safeguards of the domestic hearth, about which so much has been written, I know of none quite so sure as to marry an ugly woman. One can bind his brow with the sweet garlands of peace and security, and leave his wife behind him for two or three days with the serene confidence which a Christian feels in four aces."

REUBEN AND PHŒBE.

A PATHETIC BALLAD.

In Manchester a maiden dwelt,
Her name was Phœbe Brown,
Her cheeks were red, her hair was black,
And as she was considered by good judges to be, by all odds, the best looking girl in town.

Her age was nearly seventeen,
Her eyes were sparkling bright,
A very lovely girl she was,
And for about a year and a half there had been a young man paying attention to her by the name of Reuben Wright.

Now Reuben was a nice young man
As any in the town,
And Phœbe loved him very dear,
But, on account of his being obliged to work for a living, he never could make himself agreeable to old Mr. and Mrs. Brown.

Her cruel parents were resolved
Another she should wed,
A rich old miser in the place;
And old Brown frequently declared that rather than have his daughter marry Reuben Wright, he'd sooner knock him in the head.

But Phœbe's heart was brave and strong,
She feared not parents' frowns,
And as for Reuben Wright, so bold,
I've heard him say more than fifty times that, (with the exception of Phœbe), he didn't care a d—n for the whole race of Browns.

So Phœbe Brown and Reuben Wright
  Determined they would marry;
Three weeks ago, last Tuesday night,
  They started for old Parson Wheeler's, determined to be united in the holy bonds of matrimony, though it was tremendous dark, and rained like the Old Harry.

But Captain Brown was wide awake,
  He loaded up his gun;
And then pursued the loving pair;
  He overtook 'em when they got about half way to the Parson's, and then Reuben and Phœbe started off upon the run.

Old Brown then took a deadly aim
  Towards young Reuben's head,
But, ah! it was a bleeding shame,
  He made a mistake, and shot his only daughter, and had the unspeakable anguish of seeing her drop right down stone dead.

Then anguish filled young Reuben's heart,
  And vengeance crazed his brain,
He drew an awful jack-knife out
  And plunged it into old Brown about fifty or sixty times, so that it's very doubtful about his ever coming to again.

The briny drops from Reuben's eyes
  In torrents poured down,
He yielded up the ghost and died,
  And in this melancholy and heart-rending manner terminates the history of Reuben and Phœbe, and likewise old Captain Brown.

THE DEACON'S "INNARDS."—A worthy deacon, residing in a village not a hundred miles from Boston, one morning as he journeyed to his work, some mile or two from his home, called upon a neighbor who had just killed a hog, and bargained with him for a quantity of the pig's "innards," to be used for sausage casings, the same to be sent to his house by the neighbor's boy. As evening advanced, the deacon, who was unexpectedly detained, did not reach his home until a late hour. In the meantime his good wife, who was a very nervous woman, became very much alarmed at his non-appearance, and hastening to the door, in answer to a loud knock, was confronted by a boy holding a tin pail, which he handed to the frightened woman, exclaiming:

"Here's the deacon's guts!"

The alarm of the poor woman upon receiving the supposed contents of the deceased deacon's abdomen can be better imagined than described.

GRANT'S WHISKY.—A "Committee," just previous to the fall of Vicksburg, solicitous for the morale of our armies, took it upon themselves to visit the President, and urge the removal of General Grant.

"What for?" said Mr. Lincoln.

"Why," replied the busybodies, "he drinks too much whisky."

"Ah!" rejoined Mr. Lincoln, "can you inform me, gentlemen, where General Grant procures his whisky?"

The "committee" confessed they could not.

"Because," added Mr. Lincoln, with a twinkle in his eyes, "if I can find out I'll send every general in the field a barrel of it."

The delegation retired in reasonably good order.

THE LAWYER AND THE NUN.

THE legs of French women are justly celebrated for their beauty. Although the present Parisian taste runs a little too much *embonpoint*, Venus Gastriferia being the reigning goddess, those very useful and highly ornamental members spoken of retain only that circumference which is perfectly compatible with elegance and grace. The French people being reduced to these beautiful extremities on which to rest their claims for distinction, have consequently a language, a poetry of their own — dancing. The Gallic limb, discontented with its dark imprisonment in long skirts, has made dancing its declaration of independence, and reveals its rare proportions in terpsichorean antics. Nor does it matter under what humble or staid concealment of skirt or robe it performs its modest duty of tripping through the world; the passing wind will almost always show you the ankle, fine and firm as Diana's, swelling into a calf as round as anybody else's you choose.

At least it was such a wind that made such a revelation to M. X., a young and talented *avocat* of Paris. The last place a staid and proper man should look for a beautiful leg is under the black habit of a nun; and even if a sacrilegious mind should dare to raise the dark skirt in which so much loveliness and beauty may be buried for the still more beautiful and lovely duties of religion, a sober and well-regulated man would refuse to become aider and abettor of the accident—and therefore, as bad as if he were the prime mover in it—by permitting his eyes to rest on that beauty from which even sad garments could not take the charm. Up to the time of the above event, M. X. was a man of the highest honor and best conduct. It must have been the devil, instead of the wind, that with invisible hand flapped aside the cloth robe, and so completely overturned, by the same stroke, the self-possession of the young avocat.

It was in one of the old, narrow streets that still remain in the neighborhood of the Pantheon, and which suddenly terminate in little flights of steps, landing you in another street on another level. X. was pursuing his way along one of these antique thoroughfares when, as he was about to mount the flight of stone steps, a gust of wind—his hat was gone. He had been in a profound study, with his eyes fixed on the ground, and his hands behind him; and as he made an instinctive gesture to catch his hat, casting up his eyes at the same time, he saw—well, it does not matter what he saw. He saw what we have tried to express above; he saw that the dark disguisement of a nun's costume could not rob of its charms a beautiful ankle. The same wind that so rudely deprived him of his hat, with equal unceremoniousness raised the skirts of a *religeuse* who chanced to be mounting the little flight of steps before him.

The young *avocat* forgot his hat; he stood stupefied. And as the nun turned with a frantic movement to fight this wind—which was the devil in disguise—by holding down her robe, her young and beautiful face, full of horror at the scandal she was the unwilling instrument of, met his, and she blushed, and then became deadly pale on observing that the young *avocat* was regarding her with such rapt admiration—nothing more nor less than her legs. The expression of pain and grief on her face showed that she would rather die than be the means of causing unworthy thoughts in the mind of a fellow-creature. At least X. so interpreted her glance when their eyes met. The futility of attempting to adorn the rose or paint the lily is so generally acknowledged that it has passed into a proverb, but a beautiful leg is still more beautiful when surmounted by a beautiful and intelligent face. X. acknowledged as much by expressing more homage as he gazed into her face. "Heaven!" he thought, "hast thou made so much loveliness to be imprisoned in the life of a nun?"

It happened that near the flight of stone steps on which the above event took place, was a wine shop, before which was seated a *commissionaire.* When the latter saw the hat bounding off on the wings of the wind, he gave chase, and after capturing it, he returned to the spot where X. still stood in his surprise. If the presentation of the hat had not recalled him from his abstraction, he surely would not have followed the nun, who, with her old and wrinkled companion, was just disappearing around the corner of the street.

It would be rather the task of a romancer than of a simple reporter, to give all the curious and interesting particulars that resulted from X.'s sudden and absorbing passion for the nun. His life had heretofore been studious and well ordered; and besides being rich he was ambitious in his profession, and a bright career was prophecied for him; but he now sacrificed all to his eccentric affection. After many *demarches*, and hiring two or three *commissionaires*, he discovered that his beautiful nun was Sister Mary Augustine, and that she belonged to—well, for fear of compromising a praiseworthy order, we will call it the Sisterhood of the Solitary Sheets. Whenever she issued from the convent on her errands of mercy, she was seen by one of X.'s emissaries. At last he formed a plan for trapping the object of his affections.

One day when Sister Mary Augustine went out, accompanied by a companion on some sacred mission, she was accosted by a commissionaire.

" Sister," he said, " I am sent by a poor student who is dying from want and disease in a lodging near by. I am afraid to lose time by going further; will you come to his aid?"

They had already started on a pressing charge, and as suffering never asks unheeded of these devoted women, one continued her way, while Sister Mary accompanied the messenger to a miserable garret, where, amid all the squalid appurtenances of poverty, was X. He had employed this ruse to obtain the opportunity of declaring his love for the nun.

No one will deny that where there is a heart attainable by the eloquence of a wooer, only the homely, whose hearts are withered and whose legs are thin, are forever cold to the plea of love. In an hour's time X. had declared his feelings to such purpose that Mary Augustine's blushing and beautiful head lay weeping on his shoulder; and, following up the first happy advantage, he proposed an immediate elopement. In twenty-four hours they were in England, married. The disappearance of the nun at first caused fears of foul play, and the journals hinted at some very dreadful and mysterious doings, until the researches of the police, aided by the testimony of the *commissionaire*, showed that the only crimes in the case were the forgotten vows of Sister Mary Augustine.

A Cure for the Measles.—A lady who had two children sick with the measles, wrote to a friend for the best remedy. The friend had just received a note from another lady inquiring the way to pickle cucumbers. In the confusion, the lady who inquired about the pickles received the remedy for the measles, and the anxious mother of the six children, with horror read the following:

"Scald them three or four times in hot vinegar, and sprinkle them with salt, and in a very few days they will be cured."

A good brother, in one of the rural districts, thought he had a call to preach. Being an indifferent reader, he got a friend to read the Scripture. The chapter, on one occasion, was 22d Genesis, which contains this verse: "These eight did Milcah bear to Nahor, Abraham's brother."

On this the preacher held forth as follows:

"Brethren and sisters, let us consider our blessings. Morning and evening our wives and daughters milk our cows, and thus supply our wants; but in the days of good old Abraham, as you have just heard, it took eight to milk a bear, and they did not get much at that."

A Matter of Opinion.—A sporting Quaker puts his bets thus:

"Friend Edward, thee thinks thy horse is faster than mine. I value my opinion at $25. Now, if thee values thy opinion at the same rate, we will put the money together, and ask our horses what they think of it, and leave the conclusion to them."

AN HONEST MAN.

The admirable and beautiful lines found below are from the poems of the ancient Greek poet Philomon:

All are not just because they do no wrong;
But he who will not wrong me when he may,
He only is the truly just. I praise not them
Who, in their petty dealings, pilfer not;
But him, whose conscience spurns a secret fraud,
When he might plunder and defy surprise.
His be the praise, who, looking down with scorn
Upon the false judgment of the partial herd,
Consults his own clear heart, and boldly dares
To be, not to be thought, an honest Man!

HOW A PRIEST LOST HIS GOD.

A certain priest had horded up
  A secret mass of gold;
But where he might bestow it safe,
  By fancy was not told.
At last, it came into his head,
  To lock it in a chest,
Within the chancel; and he wrote
  Thereon, "*Hic Deus est.*"

A merry prig, whose greedy mind
  Long wish'd for such a prey,
Respected not the sacred words
  That on the casket lay.
Took out the gold, and blotted out
  The priest's inscript thereon;
Wrote "*Resurrexit non est hic,*"
  "Your God is rose and gone."

STAMPS IN HER STOCKINGS.—A gentleman was traveling in the South unattached and unincumbered, and in order to gain admission to the superior comforts of the ladies' car, he used to assist some incumbered lady traveling alone, and pay her such respectful attentions as her helpless situation seemed to require.

Once going from Jackson, Miss., to New Orleans, he had assisted a very buxom woman with a quantity of small parcels, and had otherwise rendered her such small services as any gentleman having it in his power would render to a lady traveling alone.

On arriving at New Orleans, the same attentions caused him to find himself seated next to her in the omnibus. Preparatory to starting, the conductor required his fare. When her turn came, after several mysterious struggles and plunges, with her lap full of traps, she raised her head and said:

"Mister, I guess you're a preacher, beyant ye? I guess there ain't any harm in you. When I travels, I allers carries my stamps in my stockin, 'cause you see nothing can get in there; and we are so jammed in here, that I'd thank you, old man, just to reach in for me."

WHEN Richard Pierce, printer, of Boston, worked off upon his hand-press, on the 25th of September, 1690, the first newspaper ever published in America, the Generel Court took the sheet into custody, held solemn debate over the daring disturber of the public quiet, and voted that it "contained reflections of a very high nature," and its publication was contrary to law. It was not allowed to appear again.

Smart Boy.—"My son," said a father, "take that jug, and fetch me some beer."

"Give me the money, then, father."

"My son, to get beer with money, anybody can do that—to get beer without money, that's a trick."

So the boy takes the jug, and out he goes. Shortly he returns, and places the jug before his father.

"Drink," said the son.

"How can I drink," says the father, "when there is no beer in the jug?"

"To drink beer out of a jug," says the boy, "where there is beer, anybody can do that—but to drink beer out of a jug when there is no beer, that's a trick."

The following sprightly lines were written in the choir of Rev. Dr. Scott's church, San Francisco, by the chorister, Mr. James N. Olney, and were suggested by the sight of the pews rendered vacant by the attractive eloquence of the gifted Rev. Thomas Starr King:

STARS.

The stars of heaven attract our gaze,
And charm us with their brilliant ways;
The stars of earth, fair ladies' eyes,
Control the good, the great, the wise;
To stars theatric, praise we sing;
Outshines them all the great Starr-King!
He from our Pastors lures their flocks,
And plays the deuce with the Orthodox!

A gentleman being asked why he had married so small a wife, "Why, my friend," said he, "I thought you had known, that of all evils we should choose the least."

Years ago, an old Indian, who used to travel through the country, and noted for his ready wit as a rhymester, was importuned frequently to write epitaphs. On one occasion he stopped at a farmer's, by the name of Keesel. Keesel thought it a good opportunity to secure an epitaph for his tombstone, so he asked the old man to write one for him. After the Indian had refreshed himself with a good supper, he wrote the following:

There was a man who died of late,
For whom angels did impatient wait,
With outstretched arms and wings of love,
To waft him to the realms above—

Old Keesel was delighted with the first four lines, and was anxious for the old man to finish it before retiring, but he told him he would finish it after breakfast. Keesel was wakeful all night with the beauty of his epitaph. Breakfast was ready early, and the old man summoned. After eating heartily, he put on his hat, handed Keesel the following, and started off upon a pretty fast walk:

While hovering round the lower skies,
And still watching for the prize,
In slipped the devil like a weasel,
And down to hell he kicked old Keesel.

At a proper distance the Indian ventured to look back, and saw old Keesel shaking his fist at him in a terrible passion.

Among the conditions of sale by an Irish auctioneer was the following: "The highest bidder to be purchaser, unless some gentleman bids more."

The man who makes a joke without intending it frequently amuses us more than the most ingenious of professional jokers—as when the milkman in the play is charged with putting calves' brains in his milk, he answered:

"Brains! I never had such a thing in my head!"

It was the same sort of a case when a juryman having asked the judge to excuse him from serving on account of deafness, the latter said:

"Couldn't you hear my charge to the grand jury?"

"Yes, I heard it," said the man, "but I couldn't make any sense of it?"

Some time ago, a party of theologians were at dinner, and of course the conversation at once turned upon theology. An ardent Universalist, in order to prove his faith by an illustration, took a piece of meat with his fork, and stated that he was as sure of going to heaven as he was of eating that piece of meat. As he was raising it to his mouth, it dropped from his fork under the table, and a dog swallowed it. That, however, only proved the old adage, "There is many a slip betwixt cup and lip."

A FRENCH JOKE.

THE DEAD ALIVE—A MOST EXTRAORDINARY INCIDENT IN PARISIAN LIFE.

A YOUNG man, called Arthur, was returning lately from the country to Paris, where he had been to arrange some family affairs. He was alone part of the way, but at some distance from the city a traveler got into the coach.

The traveler was a young man about the same age as Arthur, and a friendly intercourse soon sprung up between them. The new comer's name was Edward B—. He related to his fellow-traveler that he was in a most peculiar situation: he was going to be married to a lady whom he had never seen, neither did he know her father; the arrangement had been made by a friend of both parties, the preliminaries had been gone through by correspondence, and all seemed to make it a very desirable match.

On arriving in Paris, Edward and Arthur were the best friends in the world.

"I hope that we shall meet again," said the young provincial to Arthur, "and if you were not in a hurry to return home, you would do me much pleasure by breakfasting with me at the hotel where I stop."

Arthur accepted the invitation.

The young people had been hardly half an hour at table when Edward was taken suddenly with a fit, and died before assistance could be procured.

This sad occurrence threw Arthur into great consternation, and he wished at least to render a last service to the friend that he had lost, by going to inform the family in which Edward was expected of the sad catastrophe.

However, before fulfilling this sad mission, he went home to his young wife, whom he was afraid would be uneasy at his absence, so that it was not until about five in the afternoon that he was able to call upon Mr. C—.

Mr. C—, who doubted not on seeing him that he was his intended son-in-law, received him with open arms.

"How glad I am to see you, my dear Edward!" said he; "we were only waiting for you to go to dinner."

So saying, he hurried the perplexed Arthur into the dining-room, where, independent of his wife and daughter, were assembled several friends who were to be presented to the future son-in-law.

Mr. C—'s fluency of speech was so great that Arthur, not being able to get in a single word to undeceive him, was obliged to resign himself to the part forced upon him, and allowed himself to be presented to the young lady. He forgot even the death of poor Edward, and could not help smiling at the strangeness of the adventure, which was more like a scene in a farce than anything so serious as the reality.

This thought so tickled his fancy, that his spirits became excited, and he was so witty and agreeable during dinner, that everybody, including the young lady, were delighted with the supposed Edward.

At a quarter to seven, just as they were going to tea, Arthur looked at his watch, and rose.

"A thousand pardons," said he to Mr. C—, "but I am unfortunately obliged to leave you."

"Leave us, and why?"

"For an affair which does not allow of the least delay."

"What affair can you have in Paris, where you are quite a stranger?—besides, on this occasion, I quite expected that you would, at least, have devoted to us this evening."

"Impossible, my dear sir, impossible!"

"How? impossible!"

"Well," said Arthur, "since you must know all, learn that at ten o'clock this morning I arrived in Paris, and at half-past ten I died, and that as the weather is warm they mean to bury me this evening at seven o'clock. You must be aware that I cannot keep the funeral ceremony waiting; it would give them a very bad opinion of me. Besides, the Young France Hotel won't keep my body any longer."

After this speech, Arthur took his hat and vanished.

"What an original!" said Mr. C—. "Come, I shall have a very witty relation; but I wish he would have jested on a gayer subject. You see he'll be back in half an hour; I dare say he's gone to smoke a cigar on the Boulevards. This is, no doubt, the way they joke in the country."

Ten o'clock struck, and the intended had not returned.

Mr. C— became uneasy; and, to solve the mystery, went to the hotel, and inquired for Edward B—. They related to him that a traveler arrived there that morning at ten, and that half an hour after he had died, and had been buried that evening at seven; to substantiate which statement they produced the official deposition of the death of Edward B—.

Poor Mr. C— returned home in a state impossible to describe. His belief in ghosts and fetches since this occurrence remains unshaken.

TRADING HORSES.

A PIECE OF VERY SHARP PRACTICE.

GEORGE W. KENDALL writes from Texas to the *New Orleans Picayune:*

"You must all recollect little Winter, of Georgia, who used to keep a banking and lottery office at Montgomery, Alabama. Well, one afternoon, as Winter was sitting in front of his own office, a chap came cavorting up on the outside of a showy sorrel horse, head and tail up, and promptly opened, as he drew reign, with:

"'Winter, do you want a horse?'

"'No,' was the response.

"The chap put spurs to the sorrel, of course on the off side from where Mr. Winter sat, and caracoled and cavorted about the street. Finally, drawing up a second time in front of the office, he reopened with:

"'Winter, I want to sell this horse badly.'

"'What'll you take for him?' quoth Winter, jokingly.

"'One hundred and fifty dollars,' retorted the chap, putting his spur into the horse's side, and kiting about in a circle.

"'I won't give no such price,' continued Winter; "I don't want the horse, no how.'

"'What will you give for him?' queried the chap, giving him another circus turn.

"'Twenty-five dollars!' said Winter, 'and not a cent more.'

"The fellow raised himself coolly on his left foot in the stirrup, threw his right leg slowly and gracefully over the saddle and to the ground, handed the reins to Winter, and quietly said:

"'The animal is your'n; a little difference of $125 don't stop me in a horse trade just now!' and Winter was the owner of the horse.

"He sent him to a livery stable, and in about an hour the keeper came to Winter's office with 'What in the name of common sense did you send such an animal to me for? He'll poison the whole stable.'

"'What's the matter with him?' quoth Winter; 'he cavorted about lively enough when I saw him.'

"'Matter! Why, he's ring-boned, spavined, hip-shot, has the poll-evil, and may be glandered, for what I know!'

"Winter went to a book-store, laid out $2 50 for 'Youatt & Martin on the Horse,' hied to the livery stables, sat himself down, had the animal led out of his stall, and on looking him over, found he had erery disease set down in the catalogue; $25 00 for a horse, and $2 50 for book to study his ailments—a clear loss of $27 50.'"

A REMARKABLE instance of presence of mind was recently given in France. Monsieur Durand was talking with his mother-in-law, at her country chateau, when a stroke of lightning almost literally reduced her to ashes. The domestics ran into her room, when, without moving a muscle, Monsieur Durand said, "John, sweep up my mother-in-law."

Men, dying make their wills,
But wives escape a work so sad;
Why should they make what, all their lives,
The gentle dames have had?—SAXE.

A Mad Dog Story.—A good story is told of one of the baggage masters of an important station between Worcester and Boston, a fat, good natured, droll fellow, whose jokes have become quite popular on the road. His name is Bill. A short time since, while in the performance of his duties in checking baggage, an ugly little Scotch terrier got in his way, and he gave him a smart kick, which sent him over the track, yelping. The owner of the dog soon appeared in high dudgeon, wanting to know why he kicked the dog.

"Was that your dog?" asked Bill, with his usual drawl.

"Certainly, it was; what right have you to kick him?"

"He's mad," said Bill.

"No, he's not mad, either," said the owner.

"Well, I should be if anybody kicked me in that way," responded Bill.

An Enraged Editor.—Somebody has shot a dog belonging to the editor of the *Princeton* (Ky.) *Progress*, who unpacks his heart and falls to cursing in the following original vein:

"If the two-legged, bob-tailed dog that shot our four-legged, long-tailed dog on Tuesday night last, will call at our office, he can get his hide—tanned—muchly. Any one who will wait until a dark night to shoot a pup that he knows wouldn't bite any meat it thinks is alive, wouldn't hesitate to steal Blind George's last five-center, and kick the old darkey because Congress couldn't, by special enactment, make the aforesaid individual Blind George's equal—nor wouldn't dare face a white cat in a dark alley, with a brace of ten-inch navy sixes and a slung-shot."

BABY'S LETTER.

Dear old Untie,
  I dot oor letter;
My old Mammy
  She ditten better.
She every day
  Little bit stronger,
Don't mean to be sick
  Very much longer.
Daddy's so fat
  Can't hardly stagger,
Mammy says he jinks
  Too much lager!
Dear little Baby
  Had a bad colic,
Had to take *tree drops*
  Nassy paragolic!
Toot a dose of Tatnip,
  Felt worse than ever,
Shan't take no more
  Tatnip, never!
Wind on stomit,
  Felt pooty bad;
Worse fit of sitness
  Ever I had.
Ever had belly ate,
  Old Untie Bill?
Tain't no fun now,
  Say what oo will.
I used to sleep all day
  And cry all night;
Don't do so now
  Cause tain't yight!

But I'm growing,
  Getting pooty fat;
Gains most two pounds,
  Only tink o' yat!
Little femnin blankets
  Was too big before,
Nurse can't pin me
  In 'em no more.
Skirts so small,
  Baby so stout,
Had to let the plaits
  In 'em all out.
Got a head of hair
  Jess as black as night,
And big boo eyes
  Yat look very bright;
My mammy says
  Never did see
Any ozzer baby
  Half as sweet as me.
Grandma comes often,
  Aunt Sarah too;
Baby loves zem,
  Baby loves 'oo.
Baby sends a pooty kiss
  To his Unties all,
Aunties and Cousins,
  Big folks and small.
Can't yite no more,
  So good by,
Jolly ole Untie
  Wiz a glass eye!

NEVER marry a woman if she wears either black [sto]ckings or a night-cap.

A LANDLORD RETALIATED UPON.—A gentleman, well known as a New York drummer, named Frank W——, stopped for supper at the little town of Salem, Ohio, on the Pittsburgh, Fort Wayne and Chicago Railroad, a short time ago. He was hungry, and fifteen minutes was all the time allowed for refreshment. At least seven minutes had elapsed before Frank could catch the eye of the waiter, when he was furnished with a cup of coffee and a plate of beans. The beans were but half devoured, when the landlord came along and demanded a dollar. Frank protested, but the landlord was obstinate, and "all aboard!" being heard, our drummer friend was compelled to shell out. Shortly afterward, being in Cincinnati, he inquired at the telegraph office if he could send a dollar dispatch to Salem, to be paid at its destination. The clerk told him he could, when the following was sent, "C. O. D.":

CINCINNATI, December 10, 1867.

To E. M. Stone, Salem, Ohio:

I still think the price of your beans too high.

FRANK W——.

History does not record what Stone did or said on receipt of this dispatch, for which he had paid his dollar, but his feelings may be imagined.

LINES written by a lady on hearing another lady praise a certain reverend gentleman's eyes:

"I cannot praise the Doctor's eyes,
I never saw his glance divine;
For, when he prays he shuts his eyes—
And when he preaches he shuts mine!"

Patrick's Attempt at German.—Frederick the Great of Prussia had a great mania for enlisting gigantic soldiers into the Royal Guards, and paid an enormous bounty to his recruiting officers for getting them. One day the recruiting sergeant chanced to spy a Hibernian who was at least seven feet high; he accosted him in English, and proposed that he should enlist. The idea of military life and a large bounty so delighted Patrick that he immediately consented.

"But, unless you can speak German, the king will not give you so much."

"Oh," said the Irishman, "sure it's I that don't know a word of German."

"But," said the sergeant, "three words will be sufficient, and these you can learn in a short time. The king knows every man in the Guards. As soon as he sees you, he will ride up and ask you how old you are? You will say, 'Twenty-seven.' Next, how long you have been in the service? You must reply, 'Three weeks.' Finally, if you are provided with clothes and rations? You answer, 'Both.'"

Pat soon learned to pronounce his answers, but never dreamed of learning questions. In three weeks he appeared before the king in review. His majesty rode up to him. Paddy stepped forward with "present arms."

"How old are you?" said the king.

"Three weeks?" said the Irishman.

"How long have you been in the service?" asked his majesty.

"Twenty-seven years."

"Am I or you a fool?" roared the king.

"Both," replied Patrick, who was instantly taken to the guard-room, but pardoned by the king after he understood the facts of the case.

Two fast fellows, riding after a fast nag, observed a farmer sowing seed. One of them accosted him thus:

"Well, honest fellow, 'tis your business to sow, but we reap the fruits of your labor."

"'Tis very likely you may," replied the farmer, "for I am sowing hemp."

"ALL men," said Byron, "are intrinsic rascals, and I am only sorry that, not being a dog, I cannot bite them."

He also said that he had rather have a nod from an American than a snuff-box from an Emperor.

AN old proverb says, "God hath given to some men wisdom and understanding, and to others the art of playing on the fiddle."

"AN act in addition to an act"—to knock a man down, and kick him into the bargain.

WHO would believe that Edmund Burke was the originator of the phrase, "Go it, boots?"

MELANCHOLY CASE OF SUICIDE.

ON a log, sat a frog,
Crying for his daughter,
Tears he shed till his eyes were red,
And then jumped into the water—
And drowned himself.

THE world is a bundle of hay,
Mankind are the asses who pull,
Each tugs it a different way,
And the greatest of all is John Bull.—*Byron.*

"Ain't it wicked to rob dis chicken roost, Jim?"

"Dat's a great moral question, Gumbo; we isn't no time to argue it now. Hand down anodder pullet."

A son of Erin once cautioned the public against harboring or trusting his wife Peggy on his account, *as he was not married to her.*

An Irishman complained of his physician, that he kept so stuffing him with drugs that he was *sick* for a week after he was *quite well.*

Troubles are like dogs, the smaller they are the more they annoy you.

In walking, always turn your toes out and thoughts inward.

Keep aloof from quarrels—be neither a witness, nor a party.

Danger should be feared when distant, and braved when present.

A man who is not ashamed of himself, need not be ashamed of his early condition in life.

Disinterestedness is the very soul of virtue.

TO A FULL MOON.

All hail, thou glorious moon,
  Bright as a new tin pan,
Thou greatest, roundest, noblest source
  Of bread and cheese to man!

Camp-Meeting Anecdote.—At a camp-meeting, a number of ladies continued standing on the benches, notwithstanding the frequent hints from the ministers, to sit down. A reverend old gentleman, noted for his good humor, arose and said:

"I think if those ladies standing on the benches knew they had holes in their stockings, they would sit down."

This address had the desired effect—there was an immediate sinking into the seats.

A young minister standing behind him, and blushing to the temples, said:

"Oh, brother, how could you say that!"

"Say that!" said the old gentleman, "'tis a fact—if they hadn't holes in their stockings, I'd like to know how they could get them on."

Privileges of English Juries.—Juries in England have some privileges not accorded to those in this country. In a recent case at Chester, a bill of £5 for liquor and cigars consumed by the jurors was allowed by the court.

SPRING BIRDS.

The first bird of spring
Attempted to sing,
But ere he had rounded a note,
He fell from the limb—
Ah, a dead bird was him—
The music had friz in his throat.

ODE TO WINTER.

Whew!
See it snew.
Last night it blue,
And it flew,
Tew!

A Man Hanged in his Cell—He writes his own Epitaph.—Recently the boys who feed the prisoners at the county jail, Evansville, Ind., as usual visited the different cells for the purpose of giving out the regular morning rations. All the prisoners answered to "roll call," and partook of their rations, except one Mr. Trent, who was confined in jail upon a charge of having stolen a coat and pawned it to Mr. Gumberts. On reaching the cell door, the attendants were struck with horror and amazement at beholding the lifeless remains of the occupant, suspended by a rope. They quickly called the jailer, Alexander Dexter, who, with the utmost speed, hastened in search of Sheriff Miller, informing him of the fact that Trent had "shuffled off this mortal coil."

A messenger was sent in hot haste for the coroner—who was found quietly eating his breakfast—with a view of holding a coroner's inquest. In due course of time the coroner arrived, and the sheriff, jailer, and all being present, the cell of the suicide was entered by Sheriff Miller, who, in breathless silence, proceeded to examine the "cold corpus." Taking hold of the arm, to see how stiff it was, he found that it readily yielded to the touch, and upon a closer examination, he discovered that the suicide consisted of the clothes of the aforesaid Trent—hat, boots and all—stuffed and suspended to the ceiling by a rope, while the prisoner broke out in loud laughter from under the bed. Of course the curses were not loud, but deep. The prisoner had written his own "epitaph," of which the following is a true copy:

I leave you, my friends, I leave this jail,
For want of better sense (and bail);
But, friends, do not let your courage fail,
For out of this you are bound to sail.

The world did say I stole a coat,
And with old Gumberts did it soak ;
But this, my friends, treat as a goak,
And think of me and not the coat.

My friends, do not with indignation boil,
I leave you ; I was not made to toil.
I shuffled off this mortal coil,
Without the use of lard or oil.

Virtue claims me for her own,
She shall have me—she alone.

It may be proper to state here that Trent made a desperate attempt to break jail some time since, for which he was subjected to the strictest surveillance by Sheriff Miller. His last effort to escape—for doubtless that was his object—was ingenious and novel, and but for the precaution of calling the coroner and summoning a jury for a coroner's inquest, he might have escaped. The jailor is not able to see a joke in it. The sheriff considers that prisoners have no right to joke.

A Strong Affair.—Professor P—— (a distinguished musician of Philadelphia), undertook to escort a young lady, an opera, singer of some note, to the contiguous borough of Germantown, where they had been invited to dine with some friends. It was Sunday, and the party, as the surest and cheapest conveyance, determined to patronize the stage, a mode of traveling which the lady viewed with but little favor.

Before they had gone a mile on their journey, she complained of a feeling of faintness, which was succeeded by sickness at the stomach.

"Oh, heavens!" she exclaimed, throwing her head

languishingly on the professor's shoulder, "what shall I do?"

"It is very strange," mused the professor.

"Strange! oh, it is dreadful!"

"Perhaps it is the motion of the stage?"

"Oh, no, not that."

"Doubtless you have had an attack of that kind before?"

"Oh, never!" she gasped; "never—oh—ah! Why did I come?" and she almost fell fainting into the arms of the alarmed professor.

"Perhaps you have pain?"

"Not that—oh—oh!"

"What then is it like?"

"It is—ah—excuse me, professor—it is a smell! Oh, such a smell! I shall die—I shall die!"

"A smell!" uttered the thoroughly perplexed musician—"a smell! I smell nothing," and he snuffed the air to the right and left like a buffalo.

The passengers laughed and winked, but it was soon apparent that without relief the lady could not long survive.

"Air! air! air!" she gasped hysterically, as the alarmed professor threw open the window.

"Oh, it is horrible, vile, villianous!" ejaculated the opera singer, revived by the fresh air.

And thus with her handsome head thrust out of the window, she finished the unpleasant journey. Occasionally, however, her sensitive nostrils were assailed with the disagreeable odor of which she complained.

That day at dinner, she was invited to taste some fine cheese. When the plate was handed to her she turned pale.

"Take it away—take it away!" she exclaimed, "it is the horrible smell that sickened me in the stage!"

"Why, that's a good schmell," expostulated the professor; "I brought out this lump in mine pocket, as a present to our kint friends!"

The lady fainted, and the worthy professor has not been known to carry Dutch cheese in his pocket since.

WAS HE TIPSY?—An officer in Georgia relates the following conversation as occurring one evening in the army:

Artillery Captain.—"Corporal, do you see that light yonder?"

Corporal.—"Yes, sir."

Captain.—"Can't you train your gun to put a hole through it?"

Corporal.—(looking carefully through the trees in the direction of the light), "Why, Captain, that's the moon just rising."

Captain.—"Don't make a bit o' difference; put a hole right through it."

JOSEPH AND POTIPHAR'S WIFE.—An honest Dutchman in training up his son in the way he should go, frequently exercised him in Bible lessons. On one of these occasions he asked him:

"Who vas dat who vould not shleep mit Botifer's wife?"

"Shoseph."

"Dat's a coot boy! Vel, vot was de reason he would not shleep mit her?"

"Don't know—'spose he vasn't shleepy."

ITEMS FROM JOE MILLER.

"A little nonsense now and then
Is relished by the wisest men."

Three or four roguish scholars walking out one day from the University of Oxford, spied a poor fellow near Abingdon asleep in a ditch, with an ass by him, loaded with earthenware, holding the bridle in his hand: says one of the scholars to the rest, "If you will assist me, I'll help you to a little money, for you know we are bare at present." No doubt of it they were not long consenting. "Why, then," said he, "we'll go and sell this old fellow's ass at Abingdon; for you know the fair is to-morrow, and we shall meet with chapmen enough; therefore do you take the panniers off, and put them upon my back, and then lead you the ass to market, and let me alone with the old man. This being done accordingly, in a little time after, the poor man awaking, was strangely surprised to see his ass thus metamorphosed.

"Oh! for God's sake," said the scholar, "take this bridle out of my mouth, and this load from my back."

"Zoons! how came you here?" replied the old man.

"Why," said he, "my father, who is a necromancer, upon an idle thing I did to disoblige him, transformed me into an ass; but now his heart has relented, and I am come to my own shape again, I beg you will let me go home and thank him."

"By all means," said the crockery merchant; "I don't desire to have anything to do with conjuration;" and so set the scholar at liberty, who went directly to his comrades, that by this time were making merry with the money they had sold the ass for. But the old fellow was forced to go the next day to seek for a new one in the fair; and after having looked on several, his own was shown him for a very good one.

"O, ho!" said he, "what! have he and his father quarrelled again? No, no, I'll have nothing to say to him."

Gun Jones, who had made a fortune from a very mean beginning, happening to have some words with a person who had known him for some time, was asked by the other how he could have the impudence to give himself so many airs, when he knew very well that he remembered him seven years before with hardly a rag to his back.

"You lie, sirrah," replied Jones; "seven years ago I had nothing but rags to my back."

When Rabelais, the greatest droll in France, lay on his death-bed, he could not help jesting at the very last moment; for, having received the extreme unction, a friend coming to see him, said he hoped he was prepared for the next world.

"Yes, yes," replied Rabelais, "I am ready for my journey now; they have just greased my boots."

When Sir Richard Steele was fitting up his great room in York Buildings for public orations, he happened at one time to be pretty much behind-hand with his workmen, and coming one day among them, to see how they went forward, ordered one of them to get into the rostrum, and make a speech, that he might observe how it could be heard; the fellow mounting, and scratching his pate, told him he knew not what to say, for in truth he was no orator.

"Oh!" said the knight, "no matter for that; speak anything that comes uppermost."

"Why here, Sir Richard," says the fellow, "we have been working for you these six weeks, and cannot get one penny of money; pray, sir, when do you design to pay us?"

"Very well, very well," said Sir Richard; "pray come down; I have heard enough; I cannot but own you speak very distinctly, though I don't admire your subject."

A country parson having divided his text under two-and-twenty heads, one of the congregation went out of the church in a great hurry, and being met by a friend, he asked him whither he was going? "Home for my nightcap," answered the first, "for I find we are to stay here all night."

A poor man who had a termagant wife, after a long dispute, in which she was resolved to have the last word, told her, "If she spoke one more crooked word, he'd beat her brains out."

"Why, then, ram's horns, you rogue," said she, "if I die for it."

Lord Craven, in King James the First's reign, was very desirous to see Ben Jonson, which being told to Ben, he went to my lord's house; but being in a very tattered condition, as poets sometimes are, the porter refused him admittance, with some saucy language, which the other did not fail to return. My lord happening to come out while they were wrangling, asked the occasion of it? Ben, who stood in need of nobody to speak for him, said he understood his lordship desired to see him.

"You, friend?" said my lord; "who are you?"

"Ben Jonson," replied the other.

"No, no," quoth my lord, "you cannot be Ben Jonson, who wrote the 'Silent Woman;' you look as if you could not say Bo to a goose.

"Bo," cried Ben.

"Very well," said my lord, who was better pleased at the joke than offended at the affront, "I am now convinced, by your wit, you are Ben Jonson."

An Irish lawyer of the Temple, having occasion to go to dinner, left these directions in the key-hole of his door:

"I am gone to the Elephant and Castle, where you may find me; and if you can't read this note, carry it down to the stationer's, and he will read it for you."

My Lord B—— had married three wives, who were all his servants; a beggar-woman meeting him one day in the street, made him a very low curtesy.

"Ah, bless your lordship," said she, "and send you a long life; if you do but live long enough, we shall all be ladies in time."

A GENTLEMAN being at dinner at a friend's house, the first thing that came upon the table was a dish of whitings, and one being put upon his plate, he found it smell so strong, that he could not eat a bit of it; but he laid his mouth down to the fish, as if he was whispering with it, and then took up the plate, and put it to his own ear. The gentleman, at whose table he was, inquiring into the meaning, he told him that he had a brother lost at sea about a fortnight ago, and he was asking that fish if he knew anything of him.

"And what answer made he?" said the gentleman.

"He told me," replied the other, "that he could give no account of him, for he had not been at sea these three weeks."

A WITTY knave coming into a lace-shop upon Ludgate Hill, said he had occasion, for a small quantity of very fine lace, and having pitched upon that he liked, asked the woman of the shop how much she would take for as much as could reach from one of his ears to the other, and measure which way she pleased, either over his head or under his chin. After some words they agreed, and he paid the money down and began to measure, saying: "One of my ears is here, and the other is nailed to the pillory in Bristol, therefore I fear you have not enough to make good your bargain; however, I will take this piece in part, and desire you will provide the rest with all expedition."

CATO, the censor, being asked how it came to pass that he had no statue erected for him, who had so well deserved of the commonwealth? "I had rather," said he, "have this question asked, than why I had one."

A POOR dirty shoe-boy going into a church one Sunday evening, and seeing the parish boys standing in a row upon a bench to be catechized, he gets up himself, and stands in the very first place; so the parson, of course beginning with him, asked him:

"What is your name?"

"Rugged and Tough," answered he.

"Who gave you that name?" said Domine.

"Why, the boys in our alley," replied poor Rugged and Tough.

MR. G——N, the surgeon, being sent for to a gentleman who had just received a slight wound in a rencountre, gave orders to his servant to go home with all haste imaginable, and fetch a certain plaster; the patient, turning a little pale:

"Lord, sir," said he, "I hope there is no danger?"

"Yes, indeed, is there," answered the surgeon, "for if the fellow don't set up a good pair of heels, the wound will heal before he returns."

MICHAEL ANGELO, in his picture of the Last Judgment, in the Pope's chapel, painted among the figures in hell that of a certain cardinal, who, complaining to Pope Clement VII. of the affront, and desiring that it might be defaced:

"You know well," said the Pope, "I have power to deliver a soul out of purgatory, but not out of hell."

IT being proved in a trial at Guildhall, that a man's name was really Inch, who pretended it was Linch: "I see," said the judge, "the old proverb is verified in this man, who being allowed an Inch, has taken an L."

An honest French dragoon in the service of Louis the Fourteenth, having caught a man of whom he was jealous in the room with his wife, after some words, told him he would let him escape that time, but if he found him there again, he'd throw his hat out of the window. Notwithstanding this terrible threat, in a very few days he caught the spark in the same place again, and was as good as his word. Knowing what he had done, he posted away to a place where the king was, and throwing himself at his majesty's feet, implored his pardon. The king asked him what his offence was? he told the story, and how he had thrown the man's hat out of the window. "Well, well," said the king, laughing, "I very readily forgive you; considering your provocation, I think you were much in right to throw his hat out of the window." "Yes, and may it please you, my liege," said the dragoon, "but his head was in it." "Was it so," replied the king, "well, my word is passed."

Sir Thomas More, for a long time having only daughters, his wife earnestly prayed that they might have a boy; at last they had a boy, who, when he came to man's estate, proved but simple.

"Thou prayedst so long for a boy," said Sir Thomas to his wife, "that at last thou hast got one who will be a boy as long as he lives."

An extravagant young gentleman, to whom the title of lord, and a good estate, was just fallen, being a little harassed by duns, bid his steward tell them, that whilst he was a private gentleman he had leisure to run in debt, but being now advanced to a higher rank, he was too busy to pay them.

A COUNTRY curate being one Friday in Lent to examine his young catechumens, and the bell tolling for prayers, he was obliged to leave a game of all-fours unfinished, in which he had the advantage; but told his antagonist he would soon dispatch his audience, and see him out. Now, for fear any tricks should be played with the cards in his absence, he put them in his cassock; and asking one of the children how many commandments there were, which the boy, not readily answering, by accident one of the cards dropped out of his sleeve; he had the presence of mind to bid the boy take it up, and tell him what card it was, which he readily did: when turning to the parents of the child, "Are you not ashamed," said he, "to pay so little regard to the eternal welfare of your children as not to teach them their commandments? I suspected your neglect, and brought this card with me, to detect your immorality, in teaching your children to know their cards before their commandments."

A LADY whose beauty was very much upon the decline, having sent her picture to a gentleman that was to come a wooing to her, bid her chambermaid, when she was coming to dress her, take care in repairing her decays a little, or she should not look like her picture. "I warrant you, madam," says she, laying on the Bavarian red, "a little art once made your picture like you, now a little of the same art shall make you like your picture; your picture must sit to you."

A certain Irishman making love to a lady of great fortune, told her, "He could not sleep for dreaming of her."

It was a usual saying of King Charles II., that sailors got their money like horses, and spent it like asses. The following story is somewhat an instance of it; one sailor coming to see another on pay-day, desired to borrow twenty shillings of him. The moneyed man fell to telling out the sum in shillings, but a half-crown thrusting its head in, put him out, and he began to tell again; but then an impertinent crown-piece was as officious as his half brother had been, and again interrupted the tell; so that, taking up a handful of silver, he cried, "Here, Jack, give me a handful when your ship's paid, what a pox signifies counting it?"

Queen Elizabeth seeing a gentleman in her garden, who had not felt the effect of her favors so soon as he expected, looking out of her window, said to him in Italian, "What does a man think of, Sir Edward, when he thinks of nothing?" After a little pause, he answered, "He thinks, madam, of a woman's promise." The queen shrunk in her head, but was heard to say, "Well, Sir Edward, I must not confute you—anger makes dull men witty, but it keeps them poor."

One telling Charles XII. of Sweden, just before the battle of Narva, that the enemy was three to one; "I am glad to hear it," answered the king, "for then there will be enough to kill, enough to take prisoners, and enough to run away."

An Irishman getting on a high-mettled horse, it ran away with him; upon which, one of his companions called to him to stop him: "Arrah, honey," cried he, "how can I do that, when I have got no spurs?"

Soon after the death of a great officer, who was judged to have been no great advancer of the king's affairs, the king said to his solicitor Bacon, who was kinsman to that lord: "Now, Bacon, tell me truly, what say you of your cousin?" Mr. Bacon answered, "Since your majesty charges me to speak, I will deal plainly with you, and give you such a character of him, as though I was to write his history. I do think he was no fit counsellor to have made your affairs better, yet he was fit to have kept them from growing worse." "On my soul," quoth the king, "in the first thou speakest like a true man; and in the latter like a kinsman."

A sea officer, who for his courage in a former engagement, where he had lost his leg, had been preferred to the command of a good ship; in the heat of the next engagement, a cannon ball took off his wooden deputy, so that he fell upon the deck: a seaman thinking he had been fresh wounded, called out for a surgeon. "No, no," said the captain, "the carpenter will do this time."

A gentleman calling for small beer at another gentleman's table, finding it very hard, gave it the servant again without drinking. "What," said the master of the house, "don't you like the beer?" "It is not to be found fault with," answered the other, "for one should never speak ill of the dead."

Metullus Nepos, asking Cicero, the Roman orator, in a scoffing manner, "Who was his father?" Cicero replied, "Thy mother has made that question harder for thee to answer."

A CITIZEN dying greatly in debt, it coming to his creditors' ears, "Farewell," said one, "there is so much of mine gone with him." "And he carried so much of mine," said another. One hearing them make their several complaints, said, "Well, I see now, that though a man can carry nothing of his own out of the world, yet he may carry a great deal of other men's."

Two country attorneys overtaking a wagoner on the road, and thinking to break a joke upon him, asked him, "Why his fore-horse was so fat, and the rest so lean?" The wagoner knowing them to be limbs of the law, answered them, "That his fore-horse was his lawyer, and the rest were his clients."

AN Irish fellow, vaunting of his birth and family, affirmed that when he came first to England, he made such a figure, that the bells rang through all the towns he passed to London: "Ay," said a gentleman in company, "I suppose that was because you came up in a wagon with a bell-team."

A CERTAIN lord who had a termagant wife, and at the same time a chaplain who was a tolerable poet, desired him to write a copy of verses on a shrew. "I cannot imagine," said the parson, "why your lordship should want a copy, who have so good an original."

THREE gentlemen being at a tavern, whose names were Moore, Strange, and Wright; said the last: "There is but one knave in company, and that is Strange." "Yes," answered Strange, "there is one Moore." "Ay," said Moore, "that's Wright."

A Devout gentleman being very earnest in his prayers in the church, it happened that a pickpocket, being near him, stole away his watch, who, having ended his prayers, missed it, and complained to his friend that his watch was lost while he was at prayers; to which his friend replied:

"Had you watched as well as prayed, your watch had been secure;" adding these following lines:

"He that a watch will wear, this must he do,
Pocket his watch, and watch his pocket too."

A person having been put to great shifts to get money to support his credit; some of his creditors at length sent him word, that they would give him trouble. "Pshaw!" said he, "I have had trouble enough to borrow the money, and had not need be troubled to pay it again."

Sir Francis Bacon was wont to say of a passionate man, who suppressed his anger, that he thought worse than he spoke; and of an angry man, that would vent his passion in words, that he spoke worse than he thought.

The same gentleman used to say, that power in an ill man was like the power of a witch,—he could do no harm, but no good, as the magicians, said he, could turn blood into water again.

It was well answered by Archbishop Tillotson to King William, when he complained of the shortness of his sermon: "Sir," said the bishop, "could I have bestowed more time on it, it would have been shorter."

A YOUNG fellow riding down a steep hill, and doubting the foot of it was boggish, called out to a clown that was ditching, and asked him if it was hard at the bottom.

"Ay," answered the countryman, "it is hard enough at the bottom, I'll warrant you."

But in half a dozen steps the horse sunk up to the saddle skirts, which made the young gallant whip, spur, curse, and swear.

"Why, you rascal," said he to the ditcher, "didst thou not tell me it was hard at the bottom?"

"Ay," replied the other, "but you are not half way to the bottom yet."

A FRENCHMAN traveling between Dover and London, came into an inn to lodge, when the host, perceiving him a close-fisted cur, having called for nothing but a pint of beer and a pennyworth of bread to eat with a salad he had gathered by the way, resolved to fit him for it, therefore, seemingly to pay him an extraordinary respect, laid him a clean cloth for supper, and complimented him with the best bed in the house. In the morning he set a good salad before him, with cold meat, butter, etc., which provoked the monsieur to the generosity of calling for half-a-pint of wine; then coming to pay, the host gave him a bill, which for the best bed, wine, salad, and other appurtenances, he had enhanced to the value of twenty shillings.

"Vat you mean, Jernie," says the Frenchman, twenty shillings?"

But all his spluttering was in vain; for the host, with a great deal of tavern elocution, made him sensible that nothing could be abated. The monsieur, seeing no remedy but patience, seemed to pay it cheerfully. After which, he told the host that his house being extremely troubled with rats, he could give him a receipt to drive them away, so as they should never return again.

The host being very desirous to be rid of those troublesome guests, who were every day doing him one mischief or another, at length concluded to give monsieur twenty shillings for a receipt; which done, "By gar," says the monsieur, "you make all de rats one such bill as you make me, and if ever dey trouble your house again, me will be hang."

A certain lady of quality sending her Irish footman to fetch home a pair of new stays, strictly charged him to take coach if it rained, for fear of wetting them; but a great shower of rain falling, the fellow returned with the stays dripping wet; and being severely reprimanded for not doing as he was ordered to do, he said he had obeyed her orders.

"How, then," answered the lady, "could the stays be wet, if you took them into the coach with you?"

"No," replied Tague, "I know my place better; I did not go into the coach, but rode behind as I am always used to do."

The same Irishman being at a tavern, where the cook was dressing some carp, observed some of them move after they were gutted and put into the pan, which very much surprised Tague.

"Well, now, faith," said he, "of all the Christian creatures that ever I saw, this same carp will live the longest after it is dead."

Two Oxford scholars meeting on the road with a Yorkshire ostler, they fell to battering him, and told the fellow that they would prove him to be a horse or an ass.

"Well," said the ostler, "and I can prove your saddle to be a mule."

"A mule!" cried one of them, "how can that be?"

"Because," said the ostler, "it is something between a horse and an ass."

THE Trojans sending ambassadors to condole with Tiberius, upon the death of his father-in-law, Augustus, it was so long after, that the emperor hardly thought it a compliment; but told them he was likewise sorry that they had lost so valiant a knight as Hector, who was slain above a thousand years before.

A PROFLIGATE young nobleman, being in company with some sober people, desired leave to toast the devil. The gentleman who sat next to him, said:

"I have no objection to any of your lordship's friends."

A SOLDIER was bragging before Julius Cæsar of the wounds he had received in his face. Cæsar knowing him to be a coward, told him he had best take heed the next time he ran away, how he looked back.

A MELTING sermon being preached in a country church, all fell a weeping but one man, who, being asked why he did not weep with the rest? "Oh!" said he, "I belong to another parish."

The famous Jack Ogle, of facetious memory, having borrowed on note the sum of five pounds, and failing the payment, the gentlemen who had lent it indiscreetly took occasion to talk of it in the public coffee-house, which obliged Jack to take notice of it, so that it came to a challenge. Being got into the field, the gentleman, a little tender in point of courage, offered him the note to make the matter up, to which our hero consented readily, and had the note delivered:

"But now," said the gentleman, "if we should return without fighting, our companions will laugh at us; therefore, let's give one another a slight scratch, and say we wounded one another."

"With all my heart," says Jack; "come, I'll wound you first;" so drawing his sword, he whipped it through the fleshy part of his antagonist's arm, till he brought the very tears in his eyes.

This being done, and the wound tied up with a handkerchief; "Come," said the gentleman, "where shall I wound you?"

Jack, putting himself in a fighting posture, cried, "Where you can, by G—d, sir."

"Well, well," said the other, "I can swear I received this wound of you;" and so marched off contentedly.

A dog coming open-mouthed at a sergeant on a march, he ran the spear of his halbert into his throat and killed him. The owner coming out, raved extremely that his dog was killed, and asked the sergeant, "Why he could not as well have struck at him with the blunt end of the halbert?" "So I would," said he, "if he had run at me with his tail."

A RICH farmer's son, who had been bred at the University, coming home to visit his father and mother, they being one night at supper on a couple of fowls, he told them, that by logic and arithmetic he could prove those two fowls to be three. "Well, let us hear," said the old man. "Why, this," cried the scholar, "is one, and this," continued he, "is two; two and one, you know, make three." "Since you have made it out so well," answered the old man, "your mother shall have the first fowl, I will have the second, and the third you may keep yourself for your great learning."

Two countrymen, who had never seen a play in their lives, nor had any notion of it, went to the theatre in Drury Lane, when they placed themselves snug in the corner of the middle gallery; the first music played, which they liked well enough; then the second and third, to their great satisfaction; at length the curtain drew up, and three or four actors entered to begin the play; upon which one of the countrymen cried to the other, "Come, Hodge, let's be going, mayhap the gentlemen are talking about business."

A COUNTRYMAN sowing his ground, two smart fellows riding that way, called to him with an insolent air: "Well, honest fellow," said one of them, "'tis your business to sow, but we reap the fruits of your labor." To which the countryman replied, "'Tis very likely you may, truly; for I am sowing hemp."

IT was said of a person, who always ate at other people's tables, and was a great railer, that he never opened his mouth but to somebody's cost.

A YOUNG fellow having made an end of all he had, even his last suit of clothes, one said to him, "Now, I hope, you'll own yourself a happy man, for you have made an end of all your cares." "How so?" said the gentleman. "Because," said the other, "you have nothing left to take care of."

A CERTAIN justice of the peace, not far from Clerkenwell, in the first year of King George the First, when his clerk was reading a mittimus, coming to Anno Domini, 1714, "how now," cried out, with some warmth, "and why not George Domini? sure, you forget yourself strangely."

A BUTCHER that lay on his death-bed, said to his wife, "My dear, I am not a man for this world, therefore, I advise you to marry our man John." "Oh, dear husband," said she, "if that's all, never let it trouble you, for John and I have agreed that matter already."

WHEN King William, in coming from Holland, happened to meet with a violent storm at sea, the captain of the yacht cried to the chaplain, "In five minutes more, doctor, we shall be with the Lord." "The Lord forbid," answered the doctor.

A DRUNKEN fellow carrying his wife's Bible to pawn for a quartern of gin to an alehouse, the man of the house refused to take it. "What a pox," said the fellow, "will neither my word nor the word of God pass with you?"

A PROUD parson, and his man, riding over a common, saw a shepherd tending his flock, and having a new coat on, the parson asked him, in a haughty tone, who gave him that coat?

"The same," said the shepherd," that clothed you, the parish."

The parson, nettled at this, rode on a little way, and then bade his man go back, and ask the shepherd if he'd come and live with him, for he wanted a fool.

The man going accordingly to the shepherd delivered his master's message, and concluded, as he was ordered that his master wanted a fool.

"Why, are you going away, then?" said the shepherd.

"No," answered the other.

"Then, you may tell your master," replied the shepherd, "his living can't maintain three of us."

THE Lord Chief Justice Wh—d, of the King's Bench in Ireland, being esteemed a very able lawyer, and Judges C—d and B—t but very indifferent ones:

"Well," said an attorney of that court, "no bench was ever supplied like ours, for we have got a hundred judges upon it."

"A hundred!" said another, "how can that be?"

"Why," replied the first, "there is a figure of one and two ciphers."

A DYER, in a court of justice, being ordered to hold up his hand, that was all black:

"Take off your glove, friend," said the judge to him.

"Put on your spectacles, my lord," answered the dyer.

An ordinary country fellow being called as an evidence in a court of judicature, in a cause where the terms of mortgager and mortgagee were frequently used, the judge asked the countryman if he knew the difference between the mortgager and the mortgagee.

"Yes," said he, "it is the same as between the nodder and noddee."

"How is that? replied the judge.

"Why, you sit there, my lord," said the clown, "and I nod at you; then I am the nodder and your lordship is the noddee."

A celebrated M. D. coming out of a coffee-house, an impudent broken apothecary met him at the door, and accosted him with a request to lend him five guineas.

"Sir," said the doctor, "I am surprised that you should apply to me for such a favor, who do not know you!"

"Oh, dear sir," replied the apothecary, "it is for that very reason; for those who do won't lend me a farthing."

Alexander the Great asked Dionedes, a famous pirate, who was brought prisoner to him, "Why he was so bold as to rob and plunder in his seas?"

He answered, "That he did it for his profit, and as Alexander himself was used to do it. But because I do it with one single galley, I am called a pirate; but you, sire, who do it with a great army, are called a king."

This bold answer so pleased Alexander that he set him at liberty.

THE FORLORN DAMSEL.

Whilst each dear nymph is happy with her swain,
The poor Darinda sighs and sighs in vain;
Forlorn she has liv'd thrice ten revolving years,
But now, at length, a dying slave appears;
The youth raps humbly at her chamber door,
And speaks such words she never heard before.
In bed, surprised, she starts, her curtain drew,
And ask'd his will—Madam, I dye for you.
For me! a man! what does he say? he dies!
She whisks from bed, and to the toilet flies:
In haste she dress'd, but did it with an air;
And to advantage patched and comb'd her hair.
Her dying slave to rap once more presumes,
Whilst sweet Darinda washes and perfumes;
But that he might not at the door expire,
She let him in, and farther did inquire.
With cap in hand, and with submissive look,
He bow'd, and then these killing words he spoke:
Madam, I've dy'd your satin, and see here,
The black's entire, no colored stripes appear.

ON AN UGLY WOMAN IN THE DARK.

Whilst in the dark on thy soft hand I hung,
And heard the tempting syren in thy tongue;
What flames, what darts, what anguish I endured.
But, when the candle entered, I was cured.

RAISING THE WIND.

A Farce

IN TWO ACTS.

BY JAMES KENNEY.

ALSO THE STAGE BUSINESS, CHARACTERS, COSTUMES, RELATIVE POSITIONS, ETC.

CHARACTERS.

PLAINWAY,	WAITER,
FAINWOULD,	JOHN,
JEREMY DIDDLER,	MESSENGER,
SAM,	PEGGY,
RICHARD,	MISS LAURA DURABLE.

COSTUMES.

PLAINWAY.—Dark brown old man's suit, white stockings, gouty shoes.

FAINWOULD.—Dark green coat, white waistcoat, nankeen trowsers, boots.

JEREMY DIDDLER.—An old dark blue coat, torn at the elbows, and buttoned close to the throat, buff waistcoat, orange worsted pantaloons, small nankeen gaiters, shoes, old low-crowned hat.

SAM.—Drab countryman's coat, buff breeches, gray worsted stockings, countryman's hat.

RICHARD.—Gray livery coat, buff waistcoat, breeches, brown gaiters.

WAITER.—Blue coat, trowsers, white waistcoat.

JOHN.—Dark brown livery, blue stockings.

PEGGY.—White muslin dress, pink sash, black shoes.

MISS DURABLE.—Dark red muslin dress, light blue sash, cap with pink ribbons and rose.

EXITS AND ENTRANCES.

R. means *Right;* L. *Left;* R. D., *Right Door;* L. D., *Left Door*, S. E., *Second Entrance;* U. E., *Upper Entrance;* M. D., *Middle Door.*

RELATIVE POSITIONS.

R. means *Right;* L., *Left;* C., *Centre;* R. C., *Right of Centre* · L. C., *Left of Centre.*

RAISING THE WIND.

ACT I.

SCENE I.—*The Public Room in an Inn.—Two tables and three chairs.—Bell rings.*

Sam. [*Without.*] Coming, I'm coming!

Enter WAITER, R., *and* SAM, L., *meeting.*

Wai. (R.) Well, Sam, there's a little difference between this and hay-making, eh?

Sam. Yes; but I get on pretty decent, don't I? only, you see, when two or three people call at once, I'm apt to get flurried, and then I can't help listening to the droll things the young chaps say to one another at dinner—and then I don't exactly hear what they say to me, you see. Sometimes, too, I fall a laughing wi' 'em, and that they don't like, you understand.

Wai. Well, well, you'll soon get the better of all that. [*A laugh without,* R.

Sam. (L.) What's all that about?

Wai. [*Looking out.*] Oh, it's Mr. Diddler, trying to joke himself into credit at the bar. But it won't do, they know him too well.—By the by, Sam, mind you never trust that fellow.

Sam. What, him with the spy-glass?

Wai. Yes, that impudent short-sighted fellow.

Sam. Why, what for not?

Wai. Why, because he'll never pay you. The fellow lives by spunging—gets into people's houses by his songs and his bon-mots.

Sam. Bon-mots! what be they?

Wai. Why, saying smart witty things. At some of the squires' tables, he's as constant a guest as the parson or the apothecary.

Sam. Come, that's an odd line to go into, however.

Wai. Then he borrows money of everybody he meets.

Sam. Nay, but will anybody lend it him?

Wai. Why, he asks for so little at a time, that people are ashamed to refuse him; and then he generally asks for an odd sum, to give it the appearance of immediate necessity.

Sam. Damme, he must be a droll chap, however.

Wai. [*Crosses to* L.] Here he comes; mind you take care of him. [*Exit*, L.

Sam. (R.) Never you fear that, mun. I wasn't born two hundred miles north of Lunnun, to be done by Mr. Diddler, I know.

Enter DIDDLER, R.

Did. Tol lol de riddle lol:—Eh! [*Looking through a glass at Sam.*] The new waiter!—a very clod, by my hopes! an untutored clod.—My clamorous bowels, be of good cheer!—Young man, how d'ye do? Step this way, will you.—A novice, I perceive.—And how d'ye like your new line of life?

Sam. Why, very well, thank you. How do you like your old one?

Did. [*Aside.*] Disastrous accents! a Yorkshireman! —What is your name, my fine fellow?

Sam. (L.) Sam.—You needn't tell me yours—I know you, my—fine fellow!

Did. [*Aside*, R.] Oh, Fame! Fame! you incorrigible gossip!—But *nil desperandum*,—at him again! [*To Sam.*] A prepossessing physiognomy, open and ruddy, imparting health and liberality. Excuse my glass, I'm short-sighted. You have the advantage of me in that respect.

Sam. Yes, I can see as far as most folks.

Did. [*Turning away.*] Well, I'll thank ye to—oh, Sam, you haven't got such a thing as tenpence about you, have you?

Sam. Yes—[*They look at each other—Diddler expecting to receive it,*]—and I mean to keep it about me, you see.

Did. Oh—ay—certainly. I only asked for information. [*Crosses to* L.

Sam. (R.) Hark! there's the stage-coach comed in. I must go and wait upon the passengers.—You'd better ax some of them—mayhap, they mun gi' you a little better information.

Did. (L.) Stop! Harkye, Sam! you can get me some breakfast, first. I'm devilish sharp set, Sam; you see I came a long walk from over the hills, and—

Sam. Ay, and you see I come fra—Yorkshire.

Did. You do; your unsophisticated tongue declares it. Superior to vulgar prejudices, I honor you for it, for I'm sure you'll bring me my breakfast as soon as any other countryman.

Sam. Ay; well, what will you have?

Did. Anything!—tea, coffee, an egg, and so forth.

Sam. Well, now, one of us, you understand, in this transaction, mun have credit for a little while. That is, either I mun trust you for t'money, or you mun trust me for t'breakfast. Now, as you're above vulgar preju-prejudizes, and seem to be vastly taken wi' me, and, as I am not so conceited as to be above 'em, and a'n't at all taken wi' you, you'd better give me the money, you see, and trust me for t'breakfast—he! he! he!

Did. What d'ye mean by that, Sam?

Sam. Or, mayhap, you'll say me a bon-mot.

Did. Sir, your getting impertinent.

Sam. Oh, what—you don't like the terms? Why, then, as you sometimes sing for your dinner, now you may whistle for your breakfast, you see; he! he! he!

[*Exit*, R.

Did. This it is to carry on trade without a capital!—Once I paid my way, and in a pretty high road I traveled; but thou art now, Jerry Diddler, little better than a vagabond. Fie on thee! Awake thee, rouse thy spirit! honorably earn thy breakfasts and thy dinners, too. But how? my present trade is the only one that requires no apprenticeship. How unlucky, that the rich and pretty Miss Plainway, whose heart I won at Bath, should take so sudden a departure, that I should lose her address, and call myself a foolish, romantic name, that will prevent her letters from reaching me. A rich wife would pay my debts, and heal my wounded pride. But the degenerate state of my wardrobe is confoundedly against me. There's a warm old rogue, they say, with a pretty daughter, lately come to his house at the foot of the hill.—I've a great mind—it's damned impudent, but, if I hadn't surmounted my delicacy, I must have starved long ago.

Enter WAITER, L., *crosses, in haste, to* R.

George, what's the name of the new family at the foot of the hill?

Wai. I don't know: I can't attend to you now.

[*Exit*, R.

Did. There, again! Oh! I musn't bear this any longer—I must make a plunge.—No matter for the name. Gad! perhaps it may be more imposing not to know it! I'll go and scribble her a passionate billet immediately—that is, if they'll trust me with pen and ink. [*Exit*, L.

Enter FAINWOULD *and* RICHARD, R.—*Sam shows them in, crosses to* L., *and exit.*

Fain. Bring breakfast directly.—Well, Richard, I think I shall awe them into a little respect here, though they're apt to grin at me in London.

Rich. That you will, I dare say, sir.

Fain. Respect, Richard, is all I want. My father's money has made me a gentleman, and you never see any familiar jesting with your true gentlemen, I'm sure.

Rich. Very true, sir. And so, sir, you've come here to marry this Miss Plainway, without ever having seen her.

Fain. Yes; but my father and hers are very old friends; they were schoolfellows. They've lived at a distance from one another ever since, for Plainway always hated London. But my father has often visited him, and about a month ago, at Bristol, they made up this match. I didn't object to it, for my father says she is a very pretty girl; and, besides, the girls in London don't treat me with proper respect, by any means.

Rich. At Bristol?—then they're new inhabitants here. Well, sir, you must muster all your gallantry.

Fain. I will, Dick; but I'm not successful that way—I always do some stupid thing or other when I want to be attentive. The other night, in a large assembly, I picked up the tail of a lady's gown, and gave itto her for her pocket-handkerchief.—Lord, how the people did laugh!

Rich. It was an awward mistake, to be sure, sir.

Fain. Well, now for a little refreshment, and then for Miss Plainway. Go, and look after the luggage, Richard. [*Sits down.—Exit Richard,* R.

Enter DIDDLER, *with a letter in his hand,* L.

Did. Here it is, brief, but impressive. If she has but the romantic imagination of my Peggy, the direction alone must win her. [*Reads.*] "*To the Beautiful Maid at the foot of the hill.*" The words are so delicate, the arrangement so poetical, and the *tout ensemble* reads with such a languishing cadence, that a blue-stocking garden-wench must feel it! "To the Beautiful Maid at the foot of the hill." She can't resist it!

Fain. I am very hungry, I wish they would bring my breakfast. [*Sitting on* R. *of table.*

Did. Breakfast! delightful sound!—Oh! bless your unsuspicious face, we'll breakfast together. [*Diddler goes to the table, takes up a newspaper, and sits in* L. *chair.*] Sir, your most obedient. From London, sir, I presume?

Fain. At your service, sir.

Did. Pleasant traveling, sir?

Fain. Middling, sir.

Did. Any news in town, when you came away?

Fain. Not a word, sir—[*Aside.*] Come, this is polite and respectful.

Did. Pray, sir, what's your opinion of affairs in general?

Fain. Sir?—why, really, sir, — [*Aside.*] Nobody would ask my opinion in town, now.

Did. No politician, perhaps? You talked of breakfast, sir;—I was just thinking of the same thing—shall be proud of your company. [*Rises.*

Fain. [*Rises.*] You're very obliging, sir, but really I'm in such haste—

Did. Don't mention it. Company is everything to me. I'm that sort of man, that I really couldn't dispense with you.

Fain. Sir, since you insist upon it—waiter!

Sam. [*Without,* L.] Coming, sir.

Fain. Bless me, they're very inattentive here—they never bring you what you call for. [*Sits down in* R. *chair.*

Did. No, they very often serve me so!

[*Sits in chair,* L.

Enter SAM, L.

Fain. Let that breakfast be for two.

Did. Yes, this gentleman and I are going to breakfast together.

Sam. [*To Fainwould.*] You order it, do you, sir?

Fain. Yes, to be sure; didn't you hear me?

Sam. [*Chuckling.*] Yes, I heard you.

Fain. Then bring it immediately.

Sam. Yes. [*Still chuckling.*

Fain. What d'ye mean by laughing, you scoundrel?

Did. Ay, what d'ye mean by laughing, you scoundrel?

[*Drives Sam out, and follows,* L.

Fain. Now, that's disrespectful, especially to that gentleman, who seems to be so well known here; but these country waiters are always impertinent.

Enter DIDDLER, *his letter in his hand*, L.

Did. A letter for me? desire the man to wait. That bumpkin is the most impertinent—I declare it's enough to—[*Advancing towards Fainwould.*] You haven't got such a thing as half-a-crown about you, have you, sir? there's a messenger waiting, and I haven't got any change about me.

Fain. Certainly—at your service.

[*Takes out his purse, and gives him money.*

Did. I'll return it to you, sir, as soon as possible. Halloa! here!

Enter WAITER, L.

Here's the man's money—[*Putting it into his own pocket*]—bring the breakfast immediately.

Wai. Here it is, sir. [*Exit*, L.

Enter SAM, *with breakfast*, L.

Did. There we are, sir. Now, no ceremony, I beg, for I'm rather in a hurry myself. [*Exit Sam, chuckling*, L. *Diddler pours out coffee for himself.*] Help yourself, and then you'll have it to your liking. When you've done with that loaf, sir, I'll thank you for it. [*Takes it out of his hand.*] Thank you, sir. Breakfast, sir, is a very wholesome meal. [*Eating fast.*

Fain. It is, sir; I always eat a good one.

Did. So do I, sir—[*Aside,*] when I can get it.

Fain. I am an early riser, too; and in town the servants are so lazy, that I am often obliged to wait a long while before I can get any.

Did. That's exactly my case in the country.

Fain. And it's very tantalizing, when one's hungry, to be served so.

Did. Very, sir—I'll trouble you once more.

[*Snatches the bread out of his hand again.*

Fain. [*Aside.*] This can't be meant for disrespect, but it's very like it.

Did. Are you looking for this, sir? you can call for more if you want it. [*Returns a very small bit.*] Here, waiter! [*Waiter answers without.*] Some more bread for this gentleman. You eat nothing at all, sir.

Fain. Why, bless my soul, I can get nothing.

SAM *enters with rolls*, L.

Did. Very well, Sam—thank ye, Sam—but don't giggle, Sam; curse you, don't laugh. [*Following him*, L.

Sam. Ecod! you're in luck, Mr. Diddler. [*Exit*, L.

Did. [*Re-entering, and again taking his letter out of his pocket.*] What, another letter by the coach. Might I trouble you again? You haven't got such a thing as tenpence about you, have you? I live close by, sir; I'll send it to you all the moment I go home. Be glad to see you any time you'll look in, sir.

Fain. You do me honor, sir,—I haven't any half-pence; but there's my servant, you can desire him to give it you.

Did. You're very obliging. [*Puts the rolls Sam brought, unobserved, into his hat.*] I'm extremely sorry to give you so much trouble. I will take that liberty. —[*Aside.*] Come, I've raised the wind for to-day, however! Ha! ha! ha! ha! [*Exit*, R.

Fain. That must be a man of some breeding—by his ease and his impudence.

Enter SAM, L., *crossing to* R.

Who is that gentleman, waiter?

Sam. Gentleman?

Fain. Yes; by his using an inn, I suppose he lives upon his means, don't he?

Sam. Yes; but they're the oddest sort of means you ever heard of in your life. What, don't you know him?

Fain. (R.) No.

Sam. Well, I thought so.

Fain. He invited me to breakfast with him.

Sam. Ay, well, that was handsome enough.

Fain. I thought so myself.

Sam. But it isn't quite so handsome to leave you to pay for it.

Fain. Leave me to pay for it!

Sam. [*Looking out.*] Yes, I see he's off, there.

Fain. Pooh! he's only gone to pay for a letter.

Sam. A letter! bless you, there's no letter comes here for him.

Fain. Why, he's had two this morning; I lent him the money to pay for 'em.

Sam. No; did you, though?

Fain. Yes: he hadn't any change about him.

Sam. [*Laughing.*] Dam' if that an't the softest trick I ever knowed.—You come fra' Lunnun, don't you, sir?

Fain. Why, you giggling blockhead, what d'ye mean?

Sam. Why, he's had no letters, I tell you, but one he has just been writing here himself.

Fain. An impudent rascal!

Sam. Well, sir, we'll put t'breakfast all to your bill, you understand, as you ordered it.

Fain. Psha! don't tease me about the breakfast.

Sam. Upon my soul, the flattest trick I ever heard of! [*Exit, laughing*, L.

Fain. Well, this is the most disrespectful treatment.

Enter RICHARD, *meeting him*, R.

Rich. I lent that gentleman the tenpence, sir.

Fain. Confound the gentleman, and you, too!
[*Exit, driving off Richard*, R.

SCENE II.—*The Outside of Plainway's House*, R. U. E.

Enter PLAINWAY, PEGGY, *and* MISS DURABLE, R.

Miss D. (C.) Dear cousin, how soon you hurry us home.

Plain. (L.) Cousin, you grow worse and worse. You'd be gaping after the men from morning till night.

Miss D. Mr. Plainway, I tell you again, I'll not bear your sneers; though I won't blush to own, as I've often told you, that I think the society of accomplished men as innocent as it is pleasing.

Plain. Innocent enough with you it must be; but there's no occasion to stare accomplished men full in the face as they pass you, or to sit whole hours at a window to gape at them, unless it is to talk to them in your famous language of the eyes; and that, I'm afraid, few of them understand, or else you speak very badly; for, whenever you ask 'em a question in it, they never seem to make you any answer.

Miss D. Cousin Plainway, you're a sad brute, and I'll never pay you another visit while I live.

Plain. I'm afraid, cousin, you have helped my daughter to some of her wild notions. Come, knock at the door. [*Miss Durable knocks at door of house,* R. U. E.—*John opens it.*] Well, Peg, are you better prepared to meet your lover?

Peg. [*In a pensive tone and attitude.*] Alas! cruel fate ordains I shall never see him more.

[*The door opens—Miss Durable goes into the house,* R. U. E.

Plain. (L.) There—She's at her romance again. Never meet him more! why, you're going to meet him to-day for the first time.

Peg. (R.) You speak of the vulgar, the sordid Fainwould; I, of the all-accomplished Mortimer.

Plain. There! that Mortimer again.—Let me hear that name no more, hussey; I am your father, and will be obeyed.

Peg. No, sir; as Miss Somerville says, fathers of ignorant and grovelling minds, have no right to our obedience.

Plain. Miss Somerville! and who the devil is Miss Somerville?

Peg. What, sir! have you never read the Victim of Sentiment?

Plain. Damn the victim of sentiment!—Get in, you baggage—Victim of Sentiment, indeed!

[*They go into the house* R. U. E.

Enter DIDDLER L.

Did. There she dwells. Grant, my kind stars, that she may have no lover—that she may be dying for want of one; that she may tumble about in her rosy slumbers with dreaming of some unknown swain, lovely and insinuating as Jeremy Diddler. Now, how shall I get my letter delivered?

Miss D. [*Appearing at the window*, R. U. E.] Well, I declare, the balmy zephyr breathes such delightful and refreshing breezes, that, in spite of my cousin's sneers, I can't help indulging in them.

Did. [*Looking up.*] There she is, by my hopes! Ye sylphs and cupids, strengthen my sigh, that I may luxuriate on her beauties! No—not a feature can I distinguish—but she's gazing on mine, and that's enough.

Miss D. What a sweet-looking young gentleman—and his eyes are directed towards me. Oh, my palpitating heart! what can he mean?

Did. You're a made man, Jerry. I'll pay off my old scores, and never borrow another sixpence while I live.

Miss D. [*Sings.*] "Oh, listen, listen to the voice of love"—

Did. Voice indifferent:—but damn music when I've done singing for my dinners.

Enter SAM L. S. E., *with a parcel.*

Eh, Sam here—he shall deliver my letter.—My dear Sam, I'm so glad to see you.—I forgive your laughing at me.—Will you do me a favor?

Sam. If it won't take me long, for you see I've gotten a parcel to deliver in a great hurry. By the by, how nicely you did that chap.

Did. Hush, you rogue.—Look up there—do you see that lady?

Sam. Yes, I see her—

Did. Isn't she an angel?

Sam. Why, if she be, she's been a good while dead, I reckon; long enough, to appearance, to be t'mother of angels.

Did. Sam, you're a wag; but I don't understand your jokes. Now, if you can contrive to deliver this letter into her own hands, you shall be handsomely rewarded.

Sam. Handsomely rewarded!—Ay, well, let's see.—[*Takes the letter.*] "To the beauti"—

Did. Beautiful—

Sam. "Beautiful maid at the foot of the hill. [*Looks up at the window.*] Damme, now you're at some of your tricks.—[*Aside*] The old toad's got some money, I reckon. —Well, I can but try, you know; and as to the reward, why it's neither here nor there.

[*Knocks at the door—John opens it.*

Did. Thank ye, my dear fellow. Get an answer if you can, and I'll wait here for you.

[*The door opens—Sam nods and enters.*

Miss D. A letter to deliver.—Oh, dear! I'm all of a flutter. I must learn what it means.

[*Retires from the window.*

Did. Transport! she has disappeared to receive it. She's mine. Now I shall visit the country 'squires upon other terms.—I'll only sing when it comes to my turn, and never tell a story or cut a joke but at my own table. Yet I'm sorry for my pretty Peggy. I did love that little rogue; and I'm sure she never thinks of her Mortimer without sighing.—[*Sam opens the door, holds it open, and beckons.*] Eh, Sam! well, what answer? [*Sam advances*, R.

Sam. (R.) Why, first of all, she fell into a vast trepidation.

Did. (L.) Then you saw herself?

Sam. Yes, I asked to see she that were sitting at the window over the door.

Did. Well—

Sam. Well, you see, as I tell you, when she opened the letter, she fell into a vast trepidation, and fluttered and blushed, and blushed and fluttered—in short—I never see'd any person play such comical games i' my days.

Did. It was emotion, Sam.

Sam. Yes, I know it was emotion, but it was a devilish queer one. Then, at last, says she, stuttering as might be our pot-boy of a frosty morning, says she, tell your master—she thought you was my master—he! he! he!

Did. My dear Sam, go on.

Sam. Well:—tell your master, says she, that his request is rather bold, but I've too much—too much confidence in my own diss—dissension—

Did. Discretion!

Sam. Ay, I fancy you're right--in my own discretion, to be afraid of granting it. Then she turned away blushing again—

Did. Like the rose—

Sam. Like the rose, he! he! he! like a red cabbage.

Did. I'm a happy fellow.

Sam. [*Smiling.*] Why, how much did you ax her for?

Did. Only for an interview.

Sam. Oh, then you'd better go in—I ain't shut the door.

Did. I fixed it for to-morrow morning: but there's nothing like striking while the iron's hot.—I will go in, find her out, and lay myself at her feet immediately. I'll reward you, Sam, depend upon it. I shall be a moneyed man soon, and then I'll reward you. [*Sam sneers.*] I will, Sam, I give you my word. [*Goes into the house,* R. U. E.

Sam. Come, that's kind, too, to give me what nobody else will take. [*Exit,* R.

SCENE III.—*A Room in Plainway's House—Two Chairs.*

Enter DIDDLER, *cautiously,* R.

Did. Not here.—If I could but find a closet, now, I'd hide myself till she came nigh.—Luckily, here is one.—Who have we here?

[*Retires into a closet, and listens from the door in* F.

Enter FAINWOULD *and* JOHN, L.

John. (R.) Walk in, sir, I'll send my master to you, directly. *Exit,* R.

Fain. (L.) Now let me see if I can't meet with a little more respect here.

Did. [*Approaching and examining him*] My cockney friend, by Heavens! Come in pursuit of me, perhaps!

Fain. (L.) Old Plainway will treat me becomingly, no doubt; and as he positively determined with my father that I should have his daughter, I presume she's prepared to treat me with proper respect, too.

Did. (R.) What! Plainway and his daughter! Here's

a discovery! Then, my Peggy, after all, is the beautiful maid at the foot of the hill, and the sly rogue wouldn't discover herself at the window on purpose to convict me of infidelity. How unlucky! and a rival arrived, too, just at the unfortunate crisis. [*John returns* R.

John. He'll be with you immediately, Mr. Fainwould. [*Crosses, and exit,* L.

Did. Mr. Fainwould, eh!—Now, what's to be done? If I could but get rid of him, I wouldn't despair of excusing myself to Peggy.

Fain. I wonder what my father says in his letter of introduction. [*Takes a letter out of his pocket.*

Did. A letter of introduction!—Oh! oh! the first visit, then. Gad, I have it!—It's the only way; so, impudence befriend me! But, first, I'll lock the old gentleman out. [*Goes cautiously, and locks the door,* R., *whence the servant came out—then advances briskly to Fainwould.*] Sir, your most obedient.

Fain. (L.) He here!

Did. (R.) So, you've found me out, sir. But I've sent you the money—three-and-four-pence, wasn't it?—Two-and-six and ten—

Fain. Sir, I didn't mean—

Did. No, sir, I dare say not — merely for a visit. Well, I'm very glad to see you. Won't you take a seat?

Fain. And you live here, do you, sir?

Did. At present, sir, I do.

Fain. And is your name Plainway?

Did. No, sir. I'm Mr. Plainway's nephew. I'd introduce you to my uncle, but he's very busy at present with Sir Robert Rental, settling preliminaries for his marriage with my cousin.

Fain. Sir Robert Rental's marriage with Miss Plainway!

Did. Oh, you've heard a different report on that subject, perhaps. Now, thereby hangs a very diverting tale. If you're not in a hurry, sit down, and I'll make you laugh about it. [*Diddler goes up and gets a chair, which he brings forward,* R., *and, in placing it, he strikes it on Fainwould's foot.*

Fain. [*Aside.*] This is all very odd, upon my soul.

[*They sit down, he having brought down chair,* L.

Did. You see, my uncle did agree with an old fellow of the name of Fainwould, a Londoner, to marry my cousin to his son, and expects him down every day for the purpose; but, a little while ago, Sir Robert Rental, a baronet, with a thumping estate, fell in love with her, and she fell in love with him. So my uncle altered his mind, as it was very natural he should, you know, and agreed to this new match.—And, as he never saw the young cockney, and has since heard that he's quite a vulgar, conceited, foolish fellow, he hasn't thought it worth his while to send him any notice of the affair. So, if he should come down, you know, we shall have a damned good laugh at his disappointment. [*Fainwould drops his letter, which Diddler picks up unseen.*] Ha! ha! ha! Capital go, isn't it?

Fain. Ha! ha! ha! a very capital go, indeed.—[*Aside.*] Here's disrespect. But if the cockney shouldn't be disposed to think of the affair quite so merrily as you?

Did. Oh, the puppy! if he's refractory, I'll pull his nose.

Fain. [*Aside.*] Here's an impudent scoundrel! [*Rises.*] Well, I shall cheat 'em of their laugh by this meeting, however.

Did. [*Aside.*] A shy cock, I see.

Fain. Oh, you'll pull his nose, will you?

Did. If he's troublesome, I shall certainly have that pleasure. Nothing I enjoy more than pulling noses.

Fain. [*Rising.*] Sir, I wish you a good morning. Perhaps, sir, you may. [*A knocking at the door which Diddler had locked,* R.

Did. [*Aside.*] Just in time, by Jupiter!—Be quiet there. Damn that mastiff! Sir, I'm sorry you're going so soon. [*Knocking again,* R. D.] Be quiet, I say. Well, I wish you a good morning, sir! Then, you won't stay and take a bit of dinner?

Fain. Perhaps, sir, I say, you may hear from me again.

Did. Sir, I shall be extremely happy, I'm sure. [*Exit Fainwould,* L.] Bravo, Jeremy! admirably hit off! [*Knocking repeated.*] Now for the old gentleman. [*Opens the door.*

Enter PLAINWAY, R.

Plain. My dear Mr. Fainwould, I'm extremely happy to see you. I beg pardon for keeping you so long. Why, who the deuce could lock that door?

Did. He! he! he! It was I, sir.

Plain. (R.) You! why, what—

Did. (L.) A bit of humor—to show you I determined to make free, and consider myself at home.

Plain. [*Aside.*] A bit of humor! why, you must be an inveterate humorist, indeed, to begin so soon.—Well, come, that's merry and hearty.

Did. Yes, you'll find I've all that about me.

Plain. Well, and how's my old friend, and all the rest of the family?

Did. Wonderfully well, my old buck,—but here, here you have it all in black and white. [*Gives the letter.*

Plain. So, an introduction.

Did. [*Aside.*] It's rather unlucky I don't know a little more of my family. [*Struts familiarly about.*

Plain. [*Reads.*] "*This will at length introduce to you your son-in-law. I hope he will prove agreeable, both to you and your daughter. His late military habits I think have much improved his appearance, and perhaps you will already discern something of the officer about him.*" Something of the officer—[*Looking at him,*]—damme, it must be a sheriff's officer, then. "*Treat him delicately, and, above all, avoid raillery with him.*" So, then, I suppose, though he can give a joke, he can't take one.—"*It is apt to make him unhappy, as he always thinks it levelled at that stiffness in his manners, arising from his extreme timidity and bashfulness! Assure Peggy of the cordial affection of her intended father, and your faithful friend,*

"FRAS. FAINWOULD."

A very pretty introduction, truly.

Did. But where is my charming Peggy? I say—couldn't I have a little private conversation to begin with?

Plain. Why, I must introduce you, you know—I desired her to follow me—Oh! here she comes.

Did. [*Aside.*] Now, if she should fall in a passion and discover me.

Enter PEGGY, R.

Plain. My dear, this is Mr. Fainwould.

Did. Madam, your most devoted.

[*She screams—he supports her.*

Peg. [*In a low tone.*] Mortimer!

Did. [*Aside to her.*] Hush! don't be astonished—you see what I'm at—keep it up.

Plain. What ails the girl? Oh, I see, she's at her romance again.—Mr. Fainwould, try if you can't bring her about, while I go and fetch my cousin Laury to you. [*Exit*, L.

Did. No fear, sir; she is coming about. My dear Peggy! after an age of fruitless search, do I again hold you in these arms?

Peg. Cruel man! how could you torment me with so long an absence and so long a silence? I've written to you a thousand times.

Did. A thousand unlucky accidents have prevented my receiving your letters, and your address I most fatally lost not an hour after you gave it to me.

Peg. And how did you find it out at last?

Did. By an accidental rencontre with my rival. I've hummed him famously, frightened him away from the house, contrived to get his letter of recommendation, and presented myself in his stead.

Peg. It is enough to know that you are again mine; and now we'll never part.

Did. Never, if I can help it I assure you.

Peg. Lord, Mortimer, what a change there is in your dress.

Did. Eh? yes—I've dressed so on purpose; rather in the extreme, perhaps; but I thought it would look my vulgar rival better.

Peg. Well thought of; so it will. Here's my father coming back. I'd better seem a little distant, you know.

Did. You're right.

Enter PLAINWAY, L., *Diddler not seeming to notice him.*

Do, my dear lady, be merciful. But, perhaps, it is in mercy that you thus avert from me the killing lustre of those piercing eyes.

Plain. [*Aside.*] Well done, timidity.—[*To him.*] Bravo! Mr. Fainwould; you'll not be long an unsuccessful wooer, I see. Well, my cousin's coming to see you the moment she's a little composed. [*Crosses*, C.] Why, Peg, I fancy the old fool has been gaping out at window to some purpose at last. I verily believe somebody, either in jest or in earnest, has really been writing her a billet-doux, for I caught her quite in a fluster reading a letter, and the moment she saw me, she grappled it up, and her cheeks turned as red as her nose.

Did [*Much disconcerted, aside*] Oh, Lord! here's the riddle unfolded. Curse my blind eyes! what a scrape they've brought me into! a fusty old maid, I suppose. What the devil shall I do? I must humor the blunder, or she'll discover me.

Plain. Here she comes.

Did. [*Aside.*] Oh, lord! Oh, lord!

Enter MISS DURABLE, L.

Plain. Mr. Fainwould, Miss Durable.—Miss Durable, Mr. Fainwould.

[*Miss Durable screams, and seems much agitated.*

Did. [*advancing to her.*] My dear lady, what's the matter?—[*Aside to her.*] Don't be astonished. You see what I'm at—keep it up. [*Continues whispering to her.*

Plain. Why, what the devil! This fellow frightens my whole family. It must be his officer-like appearance, I suppose.

Peg. [*Aside*] Well, I declare, Laurelia means to fall in love with him, and supplant me.

Miss D. [*Aside to Diddler.*] Oh, you're a bold, adventurous man.

Did. [*To her*] Yes, I'm a very bold, adventurous man, but love, madam—

Miss D. Hush!

Plain. Why, Fainwould, you seem to make some impression upon the ladies.

Did. Not a very favorable one, it would seem, sir.

Miss D. I beg Mr. Fainwould's pardon, I'm sure. It was merely a slight indisposition, that seized me.

Plain. Oh! a slight indisposition, was it?

Peg. [*Aside.*] Yes, I see she's throwing out her lures.

Did. Will you allow me, madam, to lead you to the air? Miss Durable, here's the other arm at your service.

Miss D. [*Taking it.*] Dear sir, you're extremely obliging.

Did. Don't say so, madam; the obligation is mine.—[*Nodding.*] Plainway, you see what a way I'm in.

[*Exeunt Diddler, Peggy, and Miss Durable.*

Plain. Bashfulness!—Damme! if ever I saw such an impudent dog! [*Exit*, L.

ACT II.

Scene I.—*The Inn.*

Enter Fainwould *and* Richard, L.

Fain. In short, I never met with such disrespectful treatment since I was born:—and so the rascal's name is Diddler, is it?

Rich. So I heard the waiters call him.

Fain. As to the disappointment, Richard, it's a very fortunate one for me; for it must be a scrubby family, indeed, when one of its branches is forced to have recourse to such low practices. But, to be treated with such contempt? why am I to be laughed at every where?

Rich. If I was you, sir, I'd put that question where it's fit it should be answered.

Fain. And so I will, Richard.—If I don't go back and kick up such a bobbery—I warrant I'll—Why, he called me a vulgar, conceited, foolish cockney.

Rich. No, sure?

Fain. Yes, but he did—and what a fool my father must have been, not to see through such a set—a low-bred rascal, with his three-and-four-pence. But if I don't —I'll take your advice, Richard: I'll hire a postchaise directly, drive to the house, expose Mr. Diddler, blow up all the rest of the family, Sir Robert Rental included, and then set off for London, and turn my back upon 'em for ever. *Exeunt* R.

Enter SAM, *with a letter, followed by* MESSENGER.

Sam: Why, but what for do you bring it here?

Mes. Why, because it says, to be delivered with all possible speed. I know he comes here sometimes, and most likely won't be at home till night.

Sam. Well, if I see him, I'll gi't to him. Most likely he'll be here by and by.

Mes. Then I'll leave it. [*Exit*, R.

Sam. "Mr. Jeremiah Diddler." Dang it, what a fine seal; and I'll be shot if it don't feel like a bank note. To be delivered wi' all possible speed, too—I shouldn't wonder, now, if it brought him some good luck. Ha! ha! ha! wi' all my heart. He's a damned droll dog, and I like him vastly. [*Exit*, L.

SCENE II.—*A Room in Plainway's House.—Four Chairs.—Wine, with glasses and desert, on a table.*—PLAINWAY, C., DIDDLER, L., PEGGY, L., *and* MISS DURABLE, R., *discovered at table.*

Plain. Bravo! bravo! ha! ha! ha! [*They laugh.*

Miss D. Upon my word, Mr. Fainwould, you sing delightfully; you surely have had some practice?

Did. A little, madam.

Miss D. Well, I think it must be a very desirable accomplishment, if it were only for your own entertainment.

Did. It is in that respect, madam, that I have hitherto found it most particularly desirable.

Miss D. But surely the pleasure of pleasing your hearers—

Did. I now find to be the highest gratification it can bestow, except that of giving me a claim to a return in kind from you. [*Aside to Peggy.*] I lay it on thick, don't I?

Miss D. You really must excuse me; I can't perform to my satisfaction without the assistance of an instrument.

Plain. Well, well, cousin, then we'll hear you by and by; there's no hurry, I'm sure. Come, Mr. Fainwould, your glass is empty.

Miss D. Peggy, my love.

[*They rise to retire.—Exit Miss Durable*, R.

Plain. Peg, here, come back; I want to speak with you.

Peg. [*Returns.*] Well, papa.

Plain. Mr. Fainwould, [*They rise,*] you know I told you of a billet-doux that old Laury had received.

Peg. Yes, sir.

Plain. Coming through the passage to dinner, I picked it up.

Peg & Did. No!

Plain. Yes; I have it in my pocket—one of the richest compositions you ever beheld. I'll read it to you.

Did. [*Aside.*] How unlucky! Now, if she sees it, she'll know the hand.

Plain. [*Reads.*] "*To the beautiful maid at the foot of the hill.*" Ha! ha! ha!

Did & Peg. Ha! ha! ha! [*Diddler crosses and endeavors to keep Peggy from overlooking Plainway while he reads.*

Plain. "*Most celestial of terrestrial beings! I have received a wound from your eyes, which baffles all surgical skill. The smile of her who gave it is the only balsam that can save it. Let me, therefore, supplicate admittance to your presence to-morrow, to know at once if I may live or die.*

"*That if I'm to live, I may live your fond lover,*
And, if I'm to die, I may get it soon over.

"ADONIS."

[*They all laugh. Diddler appears much disconcerted.*

Plain. Why, this Adonis must be about as great a fool as his mistress, eh, sir? ha! ha! ha!

Did. Yes, sir; he! he! he!—[*Aside.*] They've found me out, and this is a quiz. [*Crosses*, L.

Peg. Or more likely, some poor knave, papa, that wants her money—ha! ha! ha!

Plain. Ha! ha! ha! Or, perhaps, a compound of both; eh, sir?

Did. Very likely, sir; he! he! he!—[*Aside.*] They're at me.

Plain. But we must laugh her out of the connection, and disappoint the rogue, however; though, I dare say, he little thought to create so much merriment. So short-sighted in roguery.

Did. [*Aside.*] Short-sighted! it's all up, to a certainty.

Plain. So, she's returning, impatient of being left alone, I suppose. Now, we'll smoke her.—

Did. [*Aside.*] I'll join the laugh, at all events.

Enter MISS DURABLE, R.

Miss D. Bless me, why, I'm quite forsaken among you all—

Plain. Forsaken, my dear cousin! it's only for age and ugliness to talk of being forsaken; not for a beautiful maid like you—the most celestial of terrestrial beings! [*All laugh.*

Miss D. [*Aside.*] I'm astonished—he laughing, too!

Did. [*Aside, crossing to her.*] Excuse my laughter, it's only in jest.

Miss D. In jest, sir!

Did. Yes. [*Whispers and winks.*

Plain. Well, but, my dear cousin, I hope you'll be merciful to the tender youth. Such a frown as that, now, would kill him at once.

Miss D. Cousin Plainway, this insult is intolerable. I'll not stay in your house another hour.

Plain. Nay, but, my dear Laury, I didn't expect that

truth would give offence. We'll leave Mr. Fainwould to make our peace with you.

Did. [*Aside.*] Leave me alone with her! Oh! the devil!

Peg. Ay, do, Mr. Fainwould, endeavor to pacify her —pray induce her to continue a little longer "the beautiful maid at the foot of the hill."

[*Exeunt Plainway and Peggy, through* D. F.—*Miss Durable and Diddler look sheepishly at each other.*

Did. [*Aside.*] I'm included in the quiz, as I'm a gentleman.—[*To her.*] My dear madam, how could you—

Miss D. How could I what, sir?

Did. Wear a pocket with a hole in it?

Miss D. I wear no pockets, which caused the fatal accident. But, sir, I trust it is an accident that will cause no change in your affection.

Did. [*Aside.*] Damn it! now she's going to be amorous. [*To her.*] None in the world, madam. I assure you, I love you as much as ever I did—

Miss D. I fear my conduct is very imprudent. If you should be discovered—

Did. It's not at all unlikely, madam, that I am already. [*Aside.*] Now, she'll be boring me for explanations. I must get her among them again.—[*To her.*] Or, if I'm not, if we don't take great care, I soon shall be: therefore, for better security, I think we'd better immediately join—

Miss D. Oh, dear, sir! so soon?—I declare you quite agitate me with the idea.

Did. Ma'am!

Miss D. It is so awful a ceremony, that really a little time—

Did. My dear ma'am, I didn't mean anything about a ceremony.

Miss D. Sir!

Did. You misunderstand me; I—

Miss D. You astonish me, sir! no ceremony, indeed! And would you, then, take advantage of my too susceptible heart, to ruin me? would you rob me of my innocence? would you despoil me of my honor? Cruel, barbarous, inhuman man! [*Affects to faint.*

Did. [*Supporting her*] Upon my soul, madam, I would not interfere with your honor on any account.—[*Aside.*] I must make an outrageous speech; there's nothing else will make her easy. [*Falls on his knees.*] Paragon of premature divinity! what instrument of death, or torture, can equal the dreadful power of your frowns? Poison, pistols, pikes,

[*Enter* PEGGY *at door, listening.*]

steel-traps, and spring-guns, the thumb-screw, or lead-kettle, the knout, or cat-o'-nine-tails, are impotent, compared with the words of your indignation! Cease, then, to wound by them a heart whose affection for you nothing can abate—whose—

Peg. [*Comes down,* C., *interrupting him, and showing his letter.*] So, sir, this is your fine effusion, and this is the fruit of it. False, infamous man! [*Retires up.*

Did. [*Aside to Miss Durable.*] I told you so. You'd better retire, and I'll contrive to get off. My dear Miss Plainway— [*Crosses to* C.

Peg. Don't dear me, sir—I have done with you.

Did. If you would but hear—

Peg. I'll hear nothing, sir; you can't clear yourself·

this duplicity can only arise from the meanest of motives, Mr. Mortimer.

Miss D. Mr. Mortimer! then I am the dupe, after all!

Peg. You're a mean—

Miss D. Base—

Peg. Deceitful—

Miss D. Abominable—

Did. [*Aside.*] Here's a breeze! This is raising the wind with a vengeance. My dear Miss Plainway, I—a— My dear Miss Durable—[*Aside*] pray retire; in five minutes I'll come to you in the garden, and explain all to your satisfaction.

Miss D. And, if you don't—

Did. Oh, I will; now, do go.

Peg. And you, too, madam; ar'nt you ashamed—

Miss D. Don't talk to me in that style, miss; and I shall therefore leave you with perfect indifference to make your own construction.—[*To him*] You'll find me in the garden, sir. [*Exit*, L.

Did. [*Aside.*] Floating in the fish-pond, I hope.—[*To Peggy.*] My dear Peggy, how could you for a moment believe—

Peg. I'll not listen to you—I'll go and expose you to my father immediately. He'll order the servants to toss you in a blanket, and then to kick you out of doors.

Did. [*Holding her.*] So, between two stools, poor Jeremy comes to the ground at last. Now, Peggy, my dear Peggy, I know I shall appease you. [*He takes her hand.*] That letter—I did write that letter. But, as a proof that I love you, and only you, and that I will love you as long as I live, I'll run away with you directly.

Peg. Will you, this instant?

Did. I'll hire a post-chaise immediately.—[*Aside.*] That is, if I can get credit for one.

Peg. Go, and order it.

Did. I'm off! [*Going.*] Nothing but disasters! here's the Cockney coming back in a terrible rage, and I shall be discovered.

Peg. How unlucky! Couldn't you get rid of him again?

Did. Keep out of the way, and I'll try.

[*She retires at* R. D. F.

Enter FAINWOULD, R.

Fain. So, sir—

Did. How do you do, again, sir? Hasn't my servant left you three-and-fourpence yet? Bless my soul, how stupid!

Fain. Sir, I want to see Mr. Plainway.

Did. Do you, sir? that's unlucky—he's just gone out to take a walk in the fields. Look through that window, and you may see him; there, you see, just under that hedge; now he's getting over a stile. If you like to follow him with me, I'll introduce him to you; but you'd better call again.

Fain. Sir, I see neither a hedge nor a stile, and I don't believe a word you say.

Did. [*With affected dignity.*] Don't believe a word I say, sir?

Fain. No, sir.

Did. Sir, I desire you'll quit this house.

Fain. I shan't, sir!

Did. You shan't, sir?

Fain. No, sir—my business is with Mr. Plainway. I've a post-chaise waiting for me at the door, and therefore have no time to lose.

Did. A post-chaise waiting at the door, sir?

Fain. Yes, sir; the servant told me Mr. Fainwould was within, and I'll find him, too, or I'm very much mistaken. [*Exit*, L.

Did. A post-chaise waiting at the door! we'll bribe the postboy, and jump into it.

Peg. Charming!

Did. Now, who shall I borrow a guinea of to bribe the postboy?

Enter JOHN, L.

John. Has that gentleman found my master, sir?

Did. Oh, yes, John, I showed him into the drawing-room. [*John is going.*] Stop, John, step this way. Your name is John, isn't it?

John. Yes, sir.

Did. Well, how d'ye do, John? Got a snug place here, John?

John. Yes, sir, very snug.

Did. Ay—good wages, good 'vails, eh?

John. Yes, sir, very fair.

Did. Um—you haven't got such a thing as a guinea about you, have you?

John. No, sir.

Did. Ay—that's all, John, I only asked for information. [*Exit John*, R.

Did. 'Gad—I said a civil thing or two to the gardener just now. I'll go and try him; and, to prevent all further rencontres, make my escape through the garden gate. [*Going*, L.

Enter MISS DURABLE, L.

Oh, lord! here is old innocence again.

Miss D. Well, sir, I'm all impatience for this explanation. So, you've got rid of Miss Peggy?

Did. Yes, I have pacified her, and she's retired to the —drawing-room. I was just coming to—you haven't got such a thing as a guinea about you, madam, have you? A troublesome postboy, that drove me this morning, is teasing me for his money. You see, I happened unfortunately to change my small—

Miss D. Oh! these things will happen, sir. [*Gives a purse.*] There's my purse, sir; take whatever you require.

Did. I'm robbing you, ma'am.

Miss D. Not at all—you know you'll soon return it.

Did. [*Aside.*] That's rather doubtful. [*To her.*] I'll be with you again, madam, in a moment. [*Going*, L.

Miss D. What, sir! So, even your postboys are to be attended to before me.

Did. Ma'am!

Miss D. But I see through your conduct, sir. This is a mere expedient, to avoid me again. This is too much!

Did. [*Aside.*] What the devil shall I do now? Oh! oh, dear! oh! lord!

Miss D. What's the matter?

Did. Your cruelty has so agitated me—I faint—a little water—a little water will recover me. [*Falls into a chair.*] Pray, get me a little water.

Miss D. Bless me, he's going into hysterics! Help—help—John, Betty, a little water immediately.

[*Exit*, R.—*Diddler runs off*, L.

Enter FAINWOULD, *from* L. D. F.

Fain. Nowhere to be found. So, Mr. Diddler's gone now. They've found me out by my letter, and avoid me on purpose. But I'll not stir out of the house till I see Mr. Plainway, I'm determined; so I'll sit myself quietly down. [*Sits down in the chair Diddler has left.*] I'll make the whole family treat me with a little more respect, I warrant.

Enter MISS DURABLE, *hastily*, R., *with a glass of water, which she throws in his face. She screams; he rises in a fury.*

Miss D. Here, my love—ah!

Fain. (L.) Damnation, madam! what d'ye mean?

Miss D. (R.) Oh, dear, sir! I took you for another gentleman.

Fain. Nonsense, madam! you couldn't mean to serve any gentleman in this way. Where is Mr. Plainway? I'll have satisfaction for this treatment.

Enter PLAINWAY, *through* R. D. F.

Plain. [*Comes down*, C.] Heydey! heydey! cousin; why, who is this gentleman, and what is all this noise about?

Miss D. (R.) I'm sure, cousin, I don't know who the gentleman is. All that I can explain is, that Mr. Fainwould was taken ill in that chair; that I went to get some water to recover him; and the moment after, when I came back, I found his place occupied by that gentleman.

Fain. (L.) Madam, this is no longer a time for bantering. You found Mr. Fainwould's place occupied by me, who am Mr. Fainwould; and you found him suffering no illness at all, though you wanted to give him one.

Plain. and Miss D. You Mr. Fainwould!

Fain. Yes, sir; and you've found out by this time, I suppose, that I'm perfectly acquainted with all your kind intentions towards me—that I know of your new son-in-law, Sir Robert Rental—that I am informed I am to make merriment for you—and that, if I'm refractory, your nephew, Mr. Diddler, is to pull my nose.

Plain. Sir Robert Rental, and my nephew, Mr. Diddler! Why, Laury, this is some madman broke loose. My dear sir, I haven't a nephew in the world, and never heard of such people as Sir Robert Rental or Mr. Diddler in the whole course of my life.

Fain. This is amazing!

Plain. It is, upon my soul! You say your name is Fainwould?

Fain. Certainly!

Plain. Then, nothing but the appearance of the other Mr. Fainwould can solve the riddle.

Fain. The other Mr. Fainwould?

Plain. Yes, sir; there is another gentleman so calling himself now in this house; and he was bearer of a letter of introduction from—

Fain. My letter of introduction!—The rascal picked my pocket of it, in this very house, this morning. I see through it all! I dare say your house is robbed by this time.

Plain. A villain! Why, where is he, cousin? Here, John—where are all the servants? [*Rings a bell.*

Enter JOHN, R.

Plain. Where is Mr. Fainwould?

John. What, the other, sir?

Plain. The other, sir? Then you knew this gentleman's name was Fainwould; and you never told me he was here this morning.

John. Yes, sir; I did. I sent you to him.

Plain. You sent me to the other fellow.

Plain. No, sir; I did not let in the other.

Fain. I suppose he got in at the window, then. But where is he now?

John. I am sure I don't know, sir; but I thought that gentleman was gone.

Fain. Why did you think so, sir?

John. Because, sir, the chaise is gone that you came in.

Plain. What!

Fain. Gone!

John. Yes, sir.

Plain. Why, then, the rascal's run off in it—and Peg—where is she? Where is my daughter?

Miss D. Gone with him, cousin.

John. Here they are, sir. *Exit*, R.

Enter DIDDLER, PEGGY, *and* SAM.—*Diddler dancing and singing*, R.

Plain. Sing away, my brave fellow—I'll soon change your note.

Did. Thank'ye, sir; but it's changed already. Sam, pay my debts to that young man, three-and-fourpence, [*Pointing to Fainwould,*] and give him credit for a breakfast on my account!—Ah! my dear old innocence. [*To Miss Durable.*] There's your purse again! When I'm at leisure, you shall have your explanation.

Miss D. Oh, false Adonis!

Plain. And now, sir, what have you to answer to—

Did. I plead guilty to it all. Idle habits, empty pockets, and the wrath of an offended uncle, made the shabby dog you see before you. But my angry uncle has, on his death-bed, relented. This fine, fat-headed fellow arrested our flight through the town, to put into my hand this letter, announcing the handsome bequest of ten thousand pounds, and enclosing me a hundred pound note as earnest of his sincerity.

Plain. Um!—I imagine you are the Mr. Mortimer she sometimes sighs about.

Did. The same, sir. At Bath, under that name, and under somewhat better appearances, I had the honor to captivate her.—Hadn't I, Peggy?

Peg. And isn't Mortimer your name?

Did. No, my dear; my legitimate appellation is Mr. Diddler.

Peg. What! am I to have a lover of the name of Diddler?

Sam. (R.) I'm sure Mrs. Diddler is a very pretty name.

Did. Don't be rude, Sam.

Plain. Well, sir, your promises are fair, there's no denying; but whether it would be fair to attend to them, depends entirely upon that gentleman. [*To Fainwould.*

Fain. (L.) As for me, Mr. Plainway, if your daughter has taken a fancy for another, I can't help it. Only let her refuse me respectfully, and I am satisfied.

Did. (C.) You are a very sensible fellow, and we have all a very high respect for you.

Fain. I'm satisfied.

Did. But I shall not be satisfied without the hope that

all such poor idle rogues as I have been, may learn, by my disgraceful example—

> Howe'er to vice or indolence inclined!
> By honest industry to RAISE THE WIND.

Disposition of the Characters at the Fall of the Curtain.

SAM. PLAIN. PEGGY. DID. MISS DURABLE. FAIN.
R.] L.]

THE END.

www.ingramcontent.com/pod-product-compliance
Lightning Source LLC
LaVergne TN
LVHW011223110826
845150LV00006B/1529
* 9 7 8 1 4 2 5 5 1 5 9 2 8 *